Coontail
Lagoon

Coontail Lagoon

A CELEBRATION OF LIFE

by LOUIS CASSELS

THE WESTMINSTER PRESS
Philadelphia

Book design by Dorothy Alden Smith

Published by The Westminster Press ®
Philadelphia, Pennsylvania

PRINTED IN THE UNITED STATES OF AMERICA

Library of Congress Cataloging in Publication Data

Cassels, Louis.
  Coontail Lagoon.

  1. Aiken, S. C.—Description. 2. Cassels, Louis.
I. Title.
F279.A2C37   917.5775 [B]   73–21770
ISBN 0–664–20850–9

For
the beautiful partner
whose good taste has created
and
whose company has enlivened
several happy homes,
attaining a pinnacle of achievement
at
Coontail Lagoon

A FEW PRELIMINARY WORDS
FROM THE AUTHOR TO THE READER

READERS who are familiar with my earlier books—may their days lengthen and their numbers increase—will perhaps be surprised to find that this little volume does not seem to fit into the category commonly known as "religious books."

In a way, that is true. But in a deeper sense, I feel this is the most religious book I've ever written. It deals with the profoundest theme in the Christian faith—movement from death toward life—in terms of the actual experience of a middle-aged couple.

In it, you will see a very ordinary, often weak, often frightened man crawling slowly back from the brink of death and rediscovering the sheer joy of being alive in this beautiful world that God has made.

You also will find in it an argument—one that I never expected to be making—that the truly abundant life is more freely accessible in town-and-country America than in large, cosmopolitan cities.

Between the lines, you may read still another "message" which I didn't consciously put there, but which emerged naturally from the telling of this story. This message is that the author of Proverbs 31:10–31 was absolutely right. (Please read it.)

If anyone today seriously believes that marriage is washed up as a social institution, he or she may discern in the pages that follow a great deal of testimony—all the more cogent for having been unwittingly given—that most precious asset you can possess in this world is a mate with whom you can deeply share both the adversities and the joys of life.

I suppose, when you get right down to it, that you could say this is a book about love: the love of a man and woman for each other, love of nature, love of people in their infinite variety, love of *life*.

Louis Cassels

Coontail Lagoon

PART

I

Resurrection

Sometimes decisions take shape in your mind so slowly and gradually you are unable, looking back, to fix upon any particular time when the die was cast. But I have melancholy reason to remember the exact moment when my wife, Charlotte, and I decided we'd had all we wanted of the scramble for success in big league journalism and the high-pressure life that attends it.

We were in Philadelphia, receiving one of the rewards which the world holds out as bait for diligent pursuit of the bitch goddess. Villanova University had given a dinner in my honor and was conferring on me its St. Augustine Award for distinguished service to journalism. I was sitting there at the head table, trying to look and sound modest and privately reveling in all the attention, when a reporter from the Philadelphia bureau of United Press International walked up with a stricken look on his face.

"Smitty just shot himself," he said.

Smitty was Merriman Smith, UPI's White House correspondent. He and I had been colleagues in the UPI Washington bureau for a quarter of a century, and we also were friends. Smitty was one of the best reporters who ever lived, and he had accumulated a huge pile of success symbols, including the Pulitzer Prize for his graphic eyewitness coverage of President Kennedy's assassination.

Living at top speed and working under fantastic competitive stresses (a thirty-second jump on a news bulletin about the President of the United States is regarded by a wire service as a notable triumph), Smitty wrecked his health. He became dependent on a vast pharmacopoeia of medicines, which he hauled around in a special suitcase wherever he went. And he went wherever the President went, from the era of Franklin D. Roosevelt to the first year of Richard Nixon's administration.

When no other medicine would sooth his overwrought nerves, Smitty would turn to the analgesic that has destroyed so many of the brightest and best members of our profession—booze. Eventually—in hindsight I'm almost inclined to say inevitably—he became an alcoholic. He tried hard to conquer his addiction and often managed to remain dry for months at a time. But there'd always be a relapse. He finally became so depressed about the relapses that he lay down in a bathtub at his home, placed a .357 Magnum revolver under his chin, and resigned from the rat race.

Charlotte and I sat up late that night in our room at the Bellevue-Stratford and talked about Smitty. As the initial shock wore off, I found myself wondering, not why he did it, but how he managed to keep going as long as he did. When I expressed this thought, Charlotte replied with the sudden decisiveness of a woman who has made up her mind:

"We'll move to Coontail Lagoon."

Coontail Lagoon is a cottage whose wide front deck projects over a splashing waterfall in the midst of a swamp a few miles outside of Aiken, South Carolina. We had acquired the land and built the cottage sometime before, intending to use it for a few weeks each year as a place to

12

write, or just to rest and recuperate. We loved its peace and quiet, its remoteness from the harassments of urban civilization. We especially enjoyed being close to nature—wild, unspoiled nature with all its myriad life-forms intact, going about their business in their own mysterious ways.

Living full time at Coontail Lagoon had been, until that night, a distant dream—something we looked forward to doing "someday" when we could afford to retire. Now Charlotte was saying that what we really could not afford was to wait. "Someday" would have to be now, or it might be never.

There must be some kind of extrasensory or at least subliminal communication between a man and a woman who have lived together in love for many years. In any case, it is a fact that the same thought had been forming in my own mind before she voiced it. So we didn't waste much time debating whether; the only questions to be settled were how and when.

The following week we went to New York, where I had the sad duty of substituting for Smitty as speaker at the UPI's annual breakfast for members of the American Newspaper Publishers Association in the grand ballroom of the Waldorf-Astoria. After breakfast I shared a cab with Roger Tatarian, then editor-in-chief of UPI, from the Waldorf to the Daily News Building on 42d Street, where UPI has its world headquarters.

"Roger," I said, "I want out. I'm not quite fifty years old, and I've already had one coronary and two ulcers. I am living on tranquilizers and Maalox, and I have a strong feeling that I just can't last much longer in my present job."

My title then was senior editor, but my actual job was utility outfielder. On the staff schedule sheet posted each week, my duties were described simply as "assignment," a newsroom term meaning a reporter is available to the top

13

editors for whatever chores they wish to assign to him. I covered White House press conferences, election campaigns, Presidential inaugurals, state funerals, Congressional hearings, Pentagon briefings, antiwar demonstrations, the weddings of Presidential daughters—you name it, and if it happened in Washington between 1947 and 1971, I probably was involved in some way in UPI's coverage. Occasionally I was sent out of town—to Detroit to cover a ghetto riot, to Memphis when Martin Luther King was shot, to a dozen cities from coast to coast to prepare a report on race relations. Once I even got an out-of-the-country assignment —to Rome to cover the Vatican Council. But tearing around the world really was Smitty's bag, not mine. Most of my work was done in Washington.

In addition to such spot reporting jobs as were assigned to me, I was writing what we called "in depth" features— long analytical reports on complex national issues currently in the news. Also, I wrote three columns a week—one a commentary on national affairs, the other two devoted to religious, theological, and moral issues, which are of great interest to me. Fortunately, they seem to interest a lot of other people too, for my columns caught on and became a more or less regular fixture in about five hundred newspapers.

Roger Tatarian, a good friend as well as a great editor, listened sympathetically to the proposition I laid before him during our taxi ride down Park Avenue. He suggested that I was depressed about Smitty's death and would later change my mind about wanting to gear down to a slower-paced life. But he agreed that if I persisted in this desire, UPI would permit me to move to Coontail Lagoon after the next Presidential election campaign. For a reduced salary, I would continue writing my syndicated columns and do occasional special features for UPI. It was exactly the

14

job I wanted and Charlotte and I now could translate "someday" into a definite date.

But no man can tell what the future holds. Fourteen months after my conversation with Roger, and eighteen months before the agreed date for my translation from Washington to Coontail Lagoon, something happened that made it necessary to change the timetable.

I woke up at 5:30 A.M. with a pain in the chest.

Since I had had a previous coronary, eight years before, I knew instantly what the pain signified. Coronary pain is not easily mistaken for any other kind. If you feel as though an elephant is sitting on your chest, don't call the zoo to come and get him. Call an ambulance to take you to the hospital.

I spent about a week in the intensive care unit at Suburban Hospital in Bethesda, Maryland, with oxygen tubes up my nostrils, and other tubes connecting my veins with overhanging jars of this and that. I was wired up to a gadget which kept continuous track of my pulse and blood pressure, and recorded each beat or flutter of my heart as a moving line of light on a green oscilloscope. There were eight small glass-walled rooms in the unit, spread out in a semicircle around a central control desk manned by the smartest, fastest-acting nurses I've ever seen.

If anyone's oscilloscope started making ominous pictures, the nurse on duty would hit an alarm button, and people would come pouring into the room—cardiologists, anesthesiologists, cardiac nurses—a complete medical team trained in snatching coronary patients back from the brink of death. I watched them do it half a dozen times for fellow patients, and I must confess I was a trifle disappointed that I never got to be the guest of honor. That reaction tells you something about a reporter—and may explain why we are apt to burn ourselves out at a fairly early age. We hate

15

to miss *anything*. Even when lying on my back in a coronary ward, I found myself thinking that a first-person description of a successful rescue from cardiac arrest would make a hell of a good story.

It was a story I never got to write. My recovery proceeded in dull, routine fashion. I spent a month in the hospital and six additional weeks of convalescence at home. After consulting my doctors, UPI executives decided that my move to Coontail Lagoon should take place as soon as I was able to travel.

We decided against farewell visits to the UPI office, the National Press Club, and our favorite restaurants. We also talked our neighbors out of giving us a going-away party. We felt that roots twenty-five years deep had better be pulled up abruptly, with a minimum of ceremony and as little sentimentality as possible. It was hard enough that way. But we got through it by the simple expedient of refusing to look back. By unspoken agreement, neither of us ever talked about what used to be or what might have been. We talked and planned and looked forward to what was going to be.

We left Washington on a cool September morning. A friend met us at the Columbia airport and drove us to Coontail Lagoon. When we walked into the cottage, Charlotte turned to kiss and hold me tight in her arms.

"We're home, darling," she said. "We're starting a new life, and it's going to be the best yet."

She was right.

HENRY DAVID THOREAU retreated to a woodland pond in Massachusetts. E. B. White fled the city for a saltwater farm in Maine. Joseph Wood Krutch found peace in the Arizona desert. Howard Hughes sought privacy on the top floors of luxury hotels.

When our turn came to bug out, the homing instinct led me irresistibly to a South Carolina swamp. Ever since an ancestor named Henry Cassels wangled a land grant from King George II in 1734, my family has lived along one or another of the great, wide rivers that flow through the low country of South Carolina. The flat, easily flooded bottom-lands adjacent to these rivers are called swamps, and natural-ists will tell you they constitute a unique (and now, sadly, fast-disappearing) type of ecological system.

I have been in love with swamps since I was a small boy. The plantation on which I grew up lay along the Savannah River, in the extreme western part of South Carolina. It included some three thousand acres of cypress swamp that had never been despoiled by the chain saws of lumbermen.

Those who have never had the privilege of paddling a boat through the silent fastness of a big cypress swamp may find it difficult to comprehend how anyone could feel that this is the most beautiful kind of place nature has ever managed to contrive. Most city dwellers, I have found, tend to envision swamps as loathsome places whose principal features are mud, murky water, and moccasins.

Well, you may encounter some mud (as well as dangerous pockets of quicksand) in a swamp. But there also will be hundreds of little islands and grassy hummocks that are quite dry most of the year. The slow-moving water may be black as coal, but this does not mean it is polluted or even that it is muddy. Its color comes from tannin in the bark of the cypress trees. It is fresh, pure water, with a taste vaguely reminiscent of weak tea (which also gets its color and flavor from tannin). As for the moccasins, they are there, all right; but they are even more anxious to stay out of your way than you are to have them do so. If a snake darts across the water toward your boat, it will be a brown water snake, entirely harmless unless his playfulness gives you a heart attack.

It's the trees that make a swamp so lovely. They grow right out of the black water. The big ones are bald cypress, known in the South simply as cypress. They are almost as ancient and as huge as redwoods, living for a thousand years and attaining heights of 150 feet or more. They have a distinctive shape: the base is wide-flared, ribbed with buttresses like a Gothic cathedral. From this solid foundation, a gradually tapering trunk rises straight as a plumbline, unencumbered with lower branches and terminating in a canopy of lacy conifer needles through which sunlight filters with a soft green glow.

Scattered among the cypresses are tupelo gums (also known as black gums), which comprise the "understory" of the watery forest. A tupelo may look small alongside a cypress, but it actually is a big tree in its own right, averaging about seventy feet in height at maturity. Like the cypress, it has a flared base, perhaps because nature has determined, through aeons of evolutionary experimentation, that this particular configuration is needed to give stability to a tall tree whose roots are embedded in the soft soil of a swamp bottom.

Below the green ceiling of cypress and tupelo, the islets are covered with a great variety of ferns, mosses, and tough-fibered water grasses. Here and there the basic green of the background is suddenly brightened by the blazing white of a swamp azalea, the profligate orange of honeysuckle, or the shy bluish-purple petals of a big-leaved violet that has taken root on a cypress knee.

I always think of a swamp as a silent place, because it is so blessedly remote from noises made by men. But it is a silence punctuated by the jackhammer sound of woodpeckers drilling into tree trunks in quest of grubs, the twittering of gnatcatchers and swamp canaries, and, occasionally, the high, clear, endlessly varied songs of mockingbirds. Competing with the birds as swamp musicians, and quite often outdoing them, at least in volume, are countless frogs, ranging from tiny tree frogs that make a barking sound to great long-legged bullfrogs who converse endlessly with each other about a jug of rum.

The black water abounds in fish. A red-breasted variety of sunfish known in the South as bream is the dominant species. But wherever the water broadens and deepens into a lake, you also will find largemouth bass, crappies, and catfish.

There are alligators. I hate to mention them because their presence reinforces the popular stereotype of a swamp as a sort of junior jungle. But they do exist and in South Carolina swamps, at least, they seem to be getting bigger and more numerous every year. This is good news to nature lovers, for there was a time when it seemed greedy real-estate developers would drain so much of Florida's wetlands that these huge amphibians would become extinct. I do not contend an alligator is lovely to look upon, but he is a fascinating creature, particularly when you come upon him unexpectedly in his natural habitat, and he will not harm you unless you are so exceedingly foolish as to go swimming in his particular stretch of water.

The most prevalent mammals of the swamp, by a wide margin, are squirrels. They scamper recklessly through the treetops, darting up and down the tall trunks to seize and store morsels of food, flinging themselves from one branch to another with an insouciant ease never attained by any daring young man on a flying trapeze. There are deer, racoons, bobcats, muskrats, opossums, and otters. The otters are the playboys of the swamp. They build mud slides on the riverbank and take turns doing belly floppers into the water. Once in a while you may catch a glimpse of a small bear, hastening away from any confrontation with man. In some streams, there also are beavers, which has come to be a matter of great regret to me, for reasons I'll go into later.

Anyway, you get the idea: a swamp is a special kind of place. Perhaps it isn't everyone's thing. But if you've been born and raised in swamp country, and have learned to love it in early boyhood, you will never be wholly content living in any other environment.

When we decided to flee the city, there was, unfortunately, no possibility of going home to the old family place. The U.S. Atomic Energy Commission had confiscated our plantation (and 250,000 acres of adjacent land) in 1950 as the site of its huge Savannah River Plant, which produces plutonium for hydrogen bombs. When I returned to my former home in 1970, on an AEC-guided visit, I was sickened to see that our cypress swamp was being used as a cooling basin for overheated water from the plant's nuclear reactors. The cypress trees were still standing—dead hulks rising from the water like giant tombstones. The water was still dark, but now it gave off steam, like a lake in Dante's *Inferno*.

Since we couldn't go home literally, we got as close to home as possible, searching out a much smaller piece of swampland in the same county. It took quite a while to find exactly the right spot. That we eventually did find it was due to the tireless efforts of Mrs. Eulalie Salley, a pioneer of the suffragette movement who at eighty-eight was still going strong as Aiken's leading realtor. One day, after we had experienced many disappointments, Mrs. Salley told us, "I've found the place." And she had. Charlotte and I knew the moment we saw it that this was for us. We named it Coontail Lagoon, because its waters are heavily infested with a waterweed which botanists call hornwort. It is better known to swamp dwellers as coontail moss because it closely resembles a racoon's ring-striped tail.

Coontail Lagoon consists of a few acres of high ground, heavily forested with loblolly pines; a small but beautiful lake; several small creeks; and one large creek or small river that cascades down a rocky waterfall directly in front of our cottage and rushes headlong into the swamp which begins at our doorstep.

By happy circumstance, our modest acreage adjoins ten thousand acres of swampland and forest owned by the Graniteville Company, a large textile firm. Its officers assure me they have no intention of "developing" this precious piece of virgin wilderness.

So, adding our few acres to the Graniteville Company's many acres, we have quite a respectable stretch of swamp. With the exuberant if not always skilled aid of several young boys who live in the neighborhood, I have built wooden

21

footbridges from islet to islet, so that visitors from the city may walk dry-shod at least a few hundred feet into the swamp and begin to sense its flavor. One of the trails leads to a spring which gushes, pure and sparkling, from the side of a low hill. I asked the state health department to test a sample of the water, to determine whether it was potable. Their report, which I have framed, says tersely "Coliform bacteria count: zero." That means not one germ could be found in a whole bottleful. (For your own peace of mind, don't ask the coliform count of your municipal water supply.) We have driven a three-inch steel pipe deep into the hillside to serve as a sanitary and convenient outflow for the spring, and have surrounded it with rocks and gravel. There is one modern intrusion: a paper-cup dispenser tacked to a tree, and a trash can for disposal of used cups. It is the best water I ever tasted, and it has the additional advantage of allowing me to respond literally to any guest who asks for "bourbon and branch water."

DURING the past few years, we've been treated to a spate of books and articles about "sensuality." The discussions that have come to my attention seem to be almost entirely concerned with sexual relations. I hope I shan't lay myself open to dark suspicions about Victorian hangups if I point out that sensuality involves a much broader range of pleasures than the tactile delights attending copulation. According to my well-worn American Heritage dictionary, the primary definition of "sensual" is "pertaining to or affecting any of the senses or a sense organ." By that definition, I have been wallowing in sensuality ever since we took up residence at Coontail Lagoon.

The sense which receives the greatest stimulation, perhaps, is hearing. Our swamp and its appurtenant streams and lakes are continually emitting lovely or mysterious sounds, and listening to them has become one of my most enjoyable pastimes.

My favorite sound, by far, comes from our waterfall. It isn't a very high waterfall by mountain standards. This is relatively flat country, and the water level drops no more than a dozen feet over the fifty-foot reach of stream that runs directly in front of our cottage. But the volume of water that cascades through this deep-banked cut is quite large, even in dry seasons. Above the falls, the creek is about fifteen feet wide and averages two or three feet in depth. But in the falls this stream is compressed into less than half that width, so that each drop of water seems obsessed with battering its way through the narrow opening, dashing itself recklessly against any obstacle and, if need be, leaping high into the air to seek clearance for the downstream rush. I have spent hundreds of hours studying the flow of the falls, and it dawned on me early in this perusal that the more obstacles were placed in the way of the water, the more spectacular a performance the water would give. I decided that this was a case in which man might, in all humility, do a little discreet tampering with nature. So we scoured the county for huge granite boulders that were in the way of some highway or construction project. Whenever I found one, I asked if I might haul it away, a permission that I invariably obtained, although, I fear, at the cost of convincing numerous excavating contractors they had met a madman. Tractored in and winched down to the creekbed, these laboriously gathered boulders have been tugged and pulled about until each of them contributes its unique part to the splashing and gurgling of the falls, even as an oboe, a flute, or a bass horn contributes to the music of a symphony.

The sound of the falls beats upon my ears as I write these words, and still I cannot describe it, except to say that it has the peculiar quality of being at once continuous and at the same time separable into hundreds of individual sounds. If you do not pay close attention, you simply hear a sort of roaring sound. But if you listen carefully, you can detect the splash which the water makes when it hits that big flat rock covered with green moss, or the gurgling sound that signifies it has cleared the last rock and is now tearing headlong into the deep, swirling pool at the base of the falls.

Our bedroom is directly above the noisiest part of the falls, and through its open windows I listen to the music of the water. At night, it is a soothing, soporific sound, far more effective than barbiturates in combating insomnia. (This is not mere rhetoric; it is the sober testimony of one who lived for many years with insomnia and barbiturates.) When I wake up in the morning, the first sound I hear is the waterfall, and there is something about its steady, never-ending flow that is immeasurably reassuring. No matter how hedged about with uncertainties our lives may be—and no one is more keenly conscious of the radical contingency of human existence than a cardiac patient—it is nice to know that there are continuities on which you can count. There are things that don't wear out or give out but just go on and on, tireless and inexhaustible, forever renewed, like my waterfall.

Next to the waterfall, the sounds which most gladden my heart at Coontail Lagoon are those made by birds. During our long years in the city, the only birds whose existence made an impression on me were the starlings who roosted in vast numbers along the cornices of buildings in downtown Washington. If you had asked me to describe the sound I most strongly associated with birds, I should have had to answer, if I were candid, "splat, splat, splat."

Even now, the bird sound that is most prominent in my sensual awareness is not trilling, warbling, or chirping, although we have a great deal of that at Coontail Lagoon. Perversely, I am most smitten by the staccato sound produced by woodpeckers as they drum their hard little heads against hollow trees. My bird-watching friends (I contend I am a bird-listener, not a bird-watcher, and steadfastly refuse to read the identification books people keep giving me) are unanimously of the opinion that woodpeckers make that pneumatic-drilling sound because they are in hot pursuit of grubs and insects living in dead trees or branches. Perhaps. But I have a sneaking suspicion that woodpeckers simply enjoy making a hell of a racket. I can think of no other reason why they would stage occasional assaults (usually at dawn) on the tin roof of an outbuilding which serves us as a tool shed. A woodpecker trying to drill a hole in a tin roof is not a musical sound. But it is an exuberant, carefree noise which exhilarates my sense of hearing and makes me glad that both the woodpecker and I are alive.

It is a dreadfully commonplace preference to admit, but of all the songbirds that populate our place, I most enjoy mockingbirds. Their versatility and their almost incredible capacity for mimicry are an eternal fascination to Charlotte and me. Our dog does not share our enthusiasm for mockingbirds. One resident mocker has learned to render a perfect imitation of the special sequence of notes which Charlotte whistles to call him to his dinner. When this wicked bird has nothing else to do, he amuses himself by summoning the poor dog prematurely to chow. He has trotted home so many times in vain expectation of being fed that I feel sure he knows someone is pulling his leg. I think he knows it's that mockingbird. I have seen him sitting under a tree glaring at the mockingbird and I would swear from the expression on his face that he sometimes wishes, just for a few moments, that he were a cat.

We have the good fortune to be situated in the midst of one of the principal flyways used by migratory birds in their annual movements. Because we have an abundance of water and a great many berry-bearing trees, and also, perhaps, because I do not tolerate on our place small boys with air rifles or big boys with shotguns, Coontail Lagoon is a well-established overnight stop for birds of many feathers who are flying south in the fall or north in the spring.

One day a brilliant Indian summer sun awakened me

26

earlier than usual. I put on an old pair of corduroy pants, a wool shirt, and rubber-soled shoes, and walked down the long causeway which leads from our cottage to the iron gates at the highway, where carriers leave our morning papers.

The moment I stepped out of the cottage I sensed something was different. There always are a lot of birds around, but this morning there were literally thousands of them, swooping, chirping, flitting from limb to limb and from tree to tree, occasionally making a shallow dive into the lake to gulp a drink of water, or take a quick bath, or both. I rushed back into the cottage for my field glasses—having decided on this occasion to descend from the lofty level of bird-listener to the more hackneyed role of bird-watcher—and as soon as my myopic eyes were outfitted with this optical aid, I had no difficulty recognizing our visitors. They were robins. Big, fat, healthy robins, full of zest, worms, and berries, heading south for the winter. They stripped our dogwoods and wild cherries of edible berries and by midmorning they decided it was time to move on. One by one at first, then in small groups, and finally in large whirring flights, they took off into the sky, pointing toward Florida, the Caribbean, or wherever robins go for the winter.

This was not our only such visitation. I am sure that we must have provisioned at one time or another nearly every migrating bird species listed in Roger Tory Peterson's book. But unless they are unusual in plumage or behavior, I rarely bother to look up the identity of our visitors. One flock that did send me to Mr. Peterson's omniscient guide consisted of birds that swooped and darted in such a peculiar fashion I concluded they must be chasing airborne insects invisible to me but not to them. This proved to be a lucky guess. Mr. Peterson, who is absolutely trustworthy in these

27

matters, informed me that I was watching flycatchers. I couldn't determine which of the several varieties of flycatchers we had as guests, not being very keen on fine points of identification, so I have arbitrarily decided to identify them as Greater Flycatchers. I find this an impressive title, although it does raise questions. Greater than whom or what? Greater in the sense of larger, greater in skill, or simply nobler in character than Least Flycatchers? Roger Tory Peterson, alas, provides no guidance on such questions, and I fear they do not concern him much.

I WOKE UP EARLY today—in that dark, dark hour before dawn. I couldn't go back to sleep, so I decided to get up and watch the sun rise.

It was a happy decision.

Sunrise is beautiful almost anywhere, but it's truly spectacular here at Coontail Lagoon. Our lake is fringed by tall pine and hardwood trees. The air in early autumn is crystal clear, with no smog or overcast to obscure the sky. So the sun comes up bright and clear.

For nearly an hour before the sun itself appears, the sky grows slowly but steadily brighter. This is the magic time of day that our forefathers called "first light." They had a name for it because that's when they got up to milk the cows and commence farm chores. Today, of course, few of us are up in time to see dawn, let alone the gradual brightening of the landscape which takes place in the hour before dawn.

Since it was a cool October morning, I was treated to one of my favorite sights—clouds of mist rising from the lake. This happens whenever the air is a lot cooler than the surface of the water. Although it's a perfectly natural phenomenon, in the half-light of predawn it has an eerie look.

The eastern end of the lake is guarded by trees a hundred feet tall. So my first glimpse of the rising sun comes through the trees. They provide a visual perspective which emphasizes the enormous size of the great orange ball during the first minutes after it rises majestically above the horizon. It takes nearly an hour for the sun to climb above the tops of the trees.

By this time, the golden orb seems somewhat smaller—an optical effect having to do with the atmosphere, or the curvature of the earth, or something like that. I never could get these things straight, and I don't really care much why the sun looks smaller when it's well above the horizon. All I know is: that's the way it looks.

An hour after its upper edge first peeks over the dark horizon, the rising sun loses the soft orange glow of dawn, and becomes so bright you can't look directly at it without hurting your eyes. It is now radiating solar heat—the primeval source of energy that enables our cold little planet to sustain life. The warm rays quickly dissipate the mist on the surface of the lake. The birds, who have been celebrating sunrise for more than an hour, now begin to dart about, seeking breakfast. By midmorning, on a clear day, the sky is a blue canopy specked out with puffs or streaks of white cloud.

The precise shade of blue varies with the season, the time of day, and the weather. The poets' favorite word for it is "azure." But I doubt if any technical term from the lexicon of artificial pigmentation can do justice to the reality.

It's a blue unlike any other blue, and you can stare at it for an hour and still be enchanted by it.

A solid blue sky is lovely enough. But its beauty is vastly enhanced by the kind of color contrast provided by puffy banks of white cumulus clouds.

30

Even more striking—and this demonstrates that man's touch is not always vile—are the white streaks that high-flying jet planes create with their contrails. They are like chalk marks scratched on a "blueboard."

Scientists say the blue we seem to see in the sky is a result of the vast depth of the upper atmosphere. While this explanation is doubtless correct, it leaves me wondering why anybody feels impelled to explain rather than simply enjoy a blue sky.

In the same vein, clouds can be defined as bodies of very fine droplets of water or particles of ice dispersed in the atmosphere at altitudes ranging from a few hundred feet to several miles. But who in his right mind wants to define a cloud? The only decent thing to do with a cloud is look at it and try to think who or what it resembles. This can be great sport, if you give free rein to your imagination.

This paean has been concerned, thus far, with the sky by day. The night sky sometimes is even lovelier. If there is a full or half moon, it is irradiated with soft, white light which hides any ugliness that may mar the landscape as effectively as a blanket of snow in winter. Moonlight, when very bright, causes trees and shrubs to cast a pale shadow. Usually it just turns them into silhouettes against the sky.

When there is little or no moon, stars bedeck the blue bowl of the heavenly hemisphere. Some people derive pleasure from identifying the various planets, stars and constellations. For myself, I must confess that my own familiarity with the names of the stars, acquired forty years ago for the purpose of obtaining a Boy Scout merit badge, has long since atrophied to the point where I can speak with confidence only of Orion, the Big Dipper, and the North Star.

But ignorance, happily, is no barrier to the delights of stargazing.

To look intently at a tiny spot of twinkling light and realize that it is a sun, perhaps the center of a solar system similar to ours, billions of light-years away, is to reexperience the feelings of the ancient Hebrew poet who said:

"When I look up at thy heavens, the work of thy fingers,
    the moon and the stars set in their place by thee,
    what is man that thou shouldst remember him,
        mortal man that thou shouldst care for him?"

I HAVE fallen in love with wildflowers.

I guess I've been dimly aware all my life that there are such things as flowering plants that grow in a wild, uncultivated, natural state—unplanted and untended by man.

But during my long years as a suburban gardener, the word "flower" automatically brought to my mind the thought of something planted, fed, mulched, weeded, sprayed, and otherwise pampered in hope of getting it to bring forth blossoms of the right size and color at the right time.

When dandelions bloomed on my lawn, or Japanese honeysuckle began to entwine a fence post, I rushed out with the spray tank to smite them with 2,4-D. I thought of them simply as weeds. Now I know that weed is simply an ignorant man's term for a wildflower growing where it's not wanted.

My reeducation about wildflowers began during the daily walks through the woods and around the lake which I have been taking ever since we moved to Coontail Lagoon. I walked at first because the doctor said I needed a two-mile hike every day to build up my weakened heart muscles. But what began as a medical necessity quickly turned into a hobby when I discovered wildflowers.

The first thing that strikes you about wildflowers—once you begin to notice their existence—is their incredible variety. My wildflower books (I now have a shelf full of them) tell me botanists have identified about five thousand different kinds of flowering plants in the eastern United States. Fortunately for the amateur trying to identify a specimen new to them, most of them fall into one of 86 "families" of plants.

Each family has distinctive characteristics. With effort and patience, you learn to recognize these family traits, and use them as a clue to identification. At least, they tell you where to look in Roger Tory Peterson's book for a drawing and description of the flower you've found. (This fellow Peterson, whose vast erudition in the matter of birds I mentioned earlier, seems to be a sort of Renaissance man in the world of nature. He can play any position.)

The largest family of flowering plants, numbering some seven hundred species, are those known to botanists as "composites." I'm told it's all right if laymen speak of it simply as "the daisy family." It includes the much-maligned dandelions, as well as numerous species of sunflowers, coneflowers, goldenrods, tansies, hawkweeds, wild lettuce, touch-me-nots, flame azaleas, fleabanes, asters, Joe-Pye weed, boneset, and thistles.

The typical composite has flat rays (you probably think of them as petals, but they are properly called rays) arranged in a circle around a center disk. Both the rays and the disk may be any of several colors. The disk of the black-eyed Susan is, logically, black (actually dark brown). Most sunflowers, daisies, and dandelions have green disks. Yellow is the most common color for rays, but you also find composites with white, pink, red, violet, blue, green, brown, and orange rays. And some, like thistles and boneset, have no true rays at all—just tight clusters of many hairlike or bristly flowers which usually are embraced by green bracts, as though they were wearing tight girdles.

One of my favorites is the mint family, because most of its members can be infallibly recognized by one easily spotted characteristic: they have square stems. All the mints are herbs and many give off an aromatic odor, but don't expect every species to resemble in fragrance the ones you probably know best, peppermint and spearmint.

Both peppermint and spearmint, by the way, are listed in field guides as "alien" plants. This means they are not native to America, but ran wild through our fields and forests after, as the botanists put it, "escaping from cultivation." (This terminology always conjures up in my imagination a series of mental images that only the late Walt Disney could have rendered comprehensible.) I have learned, from looking them up, that a majority of the flowers which now adorn vacant lots, road banks, and waysides in America are aliens that migrated here from Europe. It seems peculiarly appropriate that America should be flowered as well as peopled by immigrants.

Among the most commonly seen immigrant wildflowers are chicory (usually blue, but occasionally pink or white); red and white clover; Queen Anne's lace; the lovely oxeye daisy; and the several kinds of mallow. Another widely dispersed immigrant, which happens to come from Asia rather than Europe, is the day lily.

One of the most remarkable traits of wildflowers—and this seems to be particularly true of the immigrant varieties —is their ability to take root and grow even in the vacant lots of inner-city areas where no other living thing—even that durable creature, man—finds it easy to thrive. Without bees or butterflies to pollinate them, cut off from the sun by nearly perpetual smog, nourished only by rubble-strewn soil and polluted air, these urban wildflowers somehow manage to survive and bloom year after year, bravely brightening their little corners of the bleak landscape of concrete and asphalt that surrounds them.

It is in the country, of course, on roadsides, in fallow fields, and particularly along woodland trails, that you find wildflowers in the greatest number and variety.

The earliest arrivals, here at Coontail Lagoon, are the tiny, low-growing yellow flowers called "five fingers" (because they have five rays). They begin to peep through the pine straw in March. In April come violets and anemones. By May, the lagoons of our swamp are covered with the white blossoms of water lilies, floating on the surface of the water, rising and falling with the ebb and flow of the creek during dry or rainy seasons, opening their petals each morning when the sun rises, and curling up to sleep in a tight cluster when the sun goes down.

From June through September, we are awash in wildflowers, and I return from every walk in the woods bearing at least half a dozen new (to me) specimens that I've snipped. I spread them out on a table, examine them with a magnifying glass, study the arrangement of their leaves (alternate? opposite? whorled?), which is always a big help in identification, and then begin trying to track down their identities in a wildflower book. I do not know why I have this passion to put a name to each wildflower, but it is the only thing I ever do to them besides look at them and enjoy them. Some people photograph wildflowers, others try to dry or preserve them, and a determined few try to transplant them into gardens. I am content to know what to call them when we meet in the woods.

Some of the names are intriguing, to say the least. My

favorite, I think, is the hairy puccoon. It sounds like a dangerous beast, perhaps a hirsute cousin of the Abominable Snowman. In fact, it is a delicate little yellow flower of the forget-me-not family that blooms prolifically in woodlands and open fields in late spring and early summer. (There also is a hoary puccoon, which differs slightly from the hairy puccoon, which shows you how tricky this identification business can get.)

Sometimes I suspect botanists, or whoever names wildflowers, of not really liking them. Why else would a handsome orange-petaled flower be called a "hawkweed"? Surely, it was no poet who named the clammy cuphea, the wide-angled loosestrife, the lopseed, the hog peanut, the red turtlehead, or the spiny-leaved sow thistle.

By October, when the trees are flaunting russet, golden, and bronze leaves to proclaim the advent of autumn, another wildflower suddenly blossoms forth to decorate fields and woodlands with delicate, waving, yellow fronds. It is the greatly libeled goldenrod.

Goldenrods can thrive almost anywhere. You find them in every part of America, in open meadows and fields, along busy roadsides, in deserts, on mountainsides, in marshlands, and even on vacant city lots where you'd think no living thing could survive.

Unlike the many wildflowers previously mentioned which were originally immigrants from other countries, goldenrods are native-born Americans. This is a fact which DAR delegates may wish to take into account when they decide what kind of flower to wear at their next convention. A goldenrod is demonstrably more patriotic than an orchid, ladies.

Goldenrods are rarely used in corsages—or even as cut flowers for the home—because many people have the mistaken idea that they cause hay fever.

This base canard apparently originated from the fact that goldenrods come into bloom at about the same time as ragweeds. It is ragweed pollen, not goldenrod pollen, that causes allergic people to suffer in early autumn. Ragweed pollen is light and floats great distances through the air to seek out and torment hay fever victims. Goldenrod pollen is relatively heavy, does not carry very far in the air, and seldom if ever causes hay fever.

Although botanists have distinguished and named 125 different varieties of goldenrod in America, most of them share strong family characteristics which make them easy to recognize. They are usually two to four feet high, with a stout stem sprangling into small branches or flowery fronds at the top. The flowers are tiny, yellow-rayed blossoms, massed in showy clusters.

The color may range from deep yellow—i.e., golden—to very pale, almost creamy white. Some are coarse and hairy, some are delicate. Many have long, lancelike leaves, but a significant minority have rather fat, oval leaves. Most varieties give off a pungent odor, but a few are deliciously fragrant. One, called sweet goldenrod, has the scent of anise or licorice.

Wildflowers go on reproducing their kind with infinite precision generation after generation, century after century. Why? That to me is the most fascinating question about them. Why do they exist, reproduce, proliferate in spite of all obstacles that man, in his heedless pursuit of "progress," throws in their way?

Some may see in wildflowers a token of the incredible persistence, the determination to go on being, which seems to be a trait of the plant and animal kingdoms shared by all living things.

Others will shrug off the question as irrelevant and unanswerable. Still others will stare at the unplanted, untended, unfertilized, profligate loveliness of a patch of sow thistle or daisy fleabane, and say to themselves that the deepest mystery of the universe lies not in the evil and ugliness that abound in it, but rather in the goodness and beauty that persist amidst its perils, in spite of everything.

I WOULD NOT have you think that all is goldenrods and grosbeaks, pinheads and puccoons at our retreat in the swamps. We have our problem plants and creatures too.

One of our biggest headaches is commemorated in the name of our place: Coontail Lagoon. I think I mentioned earlier that coontail is the common name for an underwater moss whose proper botanical title is hornwort. It has become a prolific plant pest in southeastern streams and ponds and, once well established, is very hard to disestablish. For years before we took it over, our lake had been sorely neglected. No one did anything about the hornwort except to watch it spread until it had made swimming, boating, and fishing virtually impossible. The whole lake was choked with the stuff.

After lengthy consultation with our county farm agent—an obliging, soft-spoken man of vast and comprehensive knowledge—I learned of two relatively new herbicides that have the happy facility of killing hornwort without harming fish (or people) who are trying to use the water it infests.

When I first began spreading these herbicides from a rowboat over some of the thickest patches of hornwort, I was taken to task quite severely by a neighbor who is quite seized with what he calls "ecology." He seems to think ecology means that "Nature is sacred and must be left entirely alone." I listened patiently to his strictures until he dropped in a line about "reverence for life." This was too much, for I happened to know that he had devoted his entire career as a chemist to helping produce plutonium, the explosive which goes into hydrogen bombs. I decided he must have reverence for every form of life except human. I also decided to proceed with my herbicidal activities. Maybe I just don't dig ecology, but I cannot see why decontaminating a lake of hornwort differs in any essential way from decontaminating a river of sewage.

It has taken a long time, and many repeated applications of herbicide, but I think we've finally got the hornwort under control. There is no danger Coontail Lagoon will ever entirely lose its "raison de nom," but we've cleared the stuff out or at least inhibited its growth to the point where about 90 percent of the lake is now usable. The neighborhood kids now swim in it all summer long. The water comes from springs and is much cleaner, by health department test, than that in public or country club swimming pools. We have stocked it with fish—bream, bass, and channel catfish—generously supplied by a state fish hatchery at no charge. And we've splurged on a canoe, which is fun to paddle around on a soft summer evening.

Meanwhile, back at the creek which runs across another part of our property, we are locked in mortal combat with a colony of beavers.

Like other city dwellers whose knowledge of nature's furry creatures has been derived mostly from Disney cartoons, I had always thought of beavers as cute, industrious little creatures who have great fun building harmless little dams.

Now that I am eyeball to eyeball with beavers, I must

41

report that (1) they are not cute—they look like giant, wet rats; (2) they are not little—they weigh up to seventy pounds; (3) their dams are not harmless—they cause serious, costly flooding, and for their construction, beavers destroy hundreds of young trees.

Industrious they are. That much Disney got right. They are so confounded industrious that if you tear down one of their dams, they'll start rebuilding it before you get back to the tool shed to put your tools away.

For months now, the beavers and I have been locked in a grim test of wills. They build a dam, I tear it down, they build it back, I tear it down again. I keep hoping they'll get discouraged and move to some other creek—or some other part of this creek. They obviously keep hoping that I will go away. (I concede some justice to their position, since they were here first, and I can think of no reason why a beaver should feel bound by such documents as deeds and land titles prepared by human beings without consultation with the inhabitants of the stream affected.)

My principal objection to the beavers' beaverish activity is that they are rapidly denuding the forest along the shore of the creek. They fell wild cherry trees, beeches, young oaks, maples, and gums with reckless abandon.

The government's wildlife experts, I regret to say, have not been as helpful with the beaver problem as the county agent was with the hornwort. In fact, the only reply I could extract from the local representative of the wildlife bureau was a dogged insistence that "there are no beavers in the creeks around here." He stuck to this line until I brought a dripping-wet, 68-pound beaver which I had just killed with a rifle. I dumped the ugly creature on his desk, right on top of a pile of official papers he had been happily shuffling.

"What does that look like?" I asked.

42

"Looks like a beaver—damn big beaver at that," he conceded.

"Well," I said, "I've got a couple dozen more in my creek that are causing a lot of damage. What do you suggest I do to get rid of them?"

He studied the question from this new angle for a while and then thought of another line which was bureaucratically safe to take.

"Nothing you can do, mister. It's not the season for trapping beavers. In fact, you could get in trouble for shooting this one."

"Oh, I didn't shoot him," I said. "He got so discouraged trying to convince you wildlife experts of his existence, he killed himself."

I left him, with the beaver dripping on his papers. It's obviously going to be me against the beavers, with the government taking a neutral role at best, and maybe even siding with the beavers.

PART
II

Heaven in a Very Small Place

EACH PLACE on earth, from the humblest village to the biggest city, has for its inhabitants its own unique flavor, its own special qualities. Just as wine reflects, in its taste and bouquet, the type of grapes used, the soil in which they are grown, and the amount of sunshine and rainfall the vines receive in a particular year, a town derives its distinctive character from the interaction of several different factors, including its history, its people, the climate and geographical location.

One of the reasons we enjoy our new life at Coontail Lagoon is that it's just outside one of the most delightful towns in the world, Aiken, South Carolina. To revert to the analogy of the previous paragraph, if towns are like wines, Aiken belongs in the same class with Montrachet, La Tache, and Lafite-Rothschild.

By South Carolina standards, Aiken is not a very old town. By the time it was settled, Charleston had been in existence for 165 years.

Aiken was established in 1835 as a way station along the Charleston to Hamburg railroad, the first railroad in America to provide regular passenger and freight service with steam-powered locomotives. The town took its name from the president of the railroad, William Aiken. Two young

47

engineers on the railroad's staff, Andrew Dexter and C. O. Pascalis, laid out the plans, much as Major L'Enfant prepared the master design for Washington, D.C. L'Enfant had a passion for circles and radiating avenues. Dexter and Pascalis loved parks. So the town they designed consists of broad avenues, each of which has a pair of one-way streets divided by a wide belt of parkway. (This is the same basic design that federal engineers were to adopt 120 years later for the Interstate Highway System.)

Aiken's parkways were planted early in the town's history with hundreds of thousands of longleaf pines, magnolias, and dogwoods. After more than a century of tender nourishment, these trees have attained extraordinary size. Beneath them, scattered almost at random, grow huge banks of azaleas. Each bank is composed of a single type of azalea. But there are many different kinds of azaleas and most of them are represented in Aiken. So what you see when you drive along the parkways in spring are successive masses of azaleas in a dozen shades of pink, red, white, and lavender. If the dogwoods are in bloom at the same time—as they usually are—the beauty of the spectacle is almost overwhelming.

For the sake of variety, some of Aiken's better-known streets depart from the parkway pattern. South Boundary is a wide thoroughfare lined with ancient live oaks, whose branches meet over the middle of the street to form an arboreal arch. Whiskey Road (which got its name honestly because it was the road over which in prerailroad days whiskey was hauled from Savannah River ports to thirsty citizens of inland towns) is a winding street lined with massive magnolia trees that produce enormous white fragrant blossoms in late spring and early summer.

In a town that itself is one large garden, gardening inevitably is a popular hobby. Many Aiken homes are surrounded by magnificent gardens that are privately maintained with meticulous care. In these gardens you can find literally hundreds of varieties of azaleas, and nearly as many different kinds of camellias. The camellia has glossy green leaves and large, delicate flowers that some people (including me) consider even lovelier than roses or orchids.

For more than half a century after its establishment, Aiken remained a pretty little town of no great renown beyond its own borders. Its one claim to historical significance in this area was the Civil War battle of Aiken, in which Confederate cavalrymen under General "Fighting Joe" Wheeler administered a surprise defeat to a large force of General William Tecumseh Sherman's troops who were burning, pillaging, and raping their way through the South in order, as Sherman put it, to "teach these rebels that war is hell." Because Fighting Joe Wheeler chose to stand and fight before Aiken, Sherman had to make a wide detour, and Aiken was spared the destruction that befell so many South Carolina and Georgia towns during Sherman's march.

Permit me to digress here for a moment to relate an incident of family history which, I think, tells a good deal about southerners and their view of what many of them still insist on calling The War Between the States.

When I was a boy, my grandmother gave me a vivid account of the infamies which attended Sherman's application of scorched earth tactics to the southern home front. When Sherman's men arrived at our plantation (miles outside Aiken on the Savannah River), they opened fire on my great-grandmother and wounded her in the arm. It was not until years later that I learned why those damyankees shot Great-grandma. The old girl was firing at *them* from an upstairs window, and brought down three Union soldiers before they winged her. I confronted Grandmother

49

with this detail of the story which she had omitted, and she dismissed it as entirely irrelevant. "No *gentleman*," she said severely, "would return the fire of a lady."

In the period following the war, Aiken and its surrounding cotton plantations experienced the poverty that afflicted the entire South. Black people, freed from slavery, drifted northward toward cities looking for jobs, or remained at home to farm small plots on a sharecrop basis that was very close to peonage. Many once-wealthy white families had lost not only their fortunes but also most of their menfolk in the war. It is one thing to read in history books of the South's terrible losses in the war. It strikes you with much greater force to read in the pages of an old family Bible that your great-grandfather lost an arm at Antietam, but was considered the "lucky" son because he finally came home alive. All three of his brothers were killed on battlefields ranging from Shiloh to Gettysburg.

In 1890, Aiken entered a golden era which lasted for half a century, and which still sheds a somewhat dimmed radiance over the town. It resulted from a combination of climate, geology, and the contagious enthusiasm of a great woman.

The important thing about Aiken's climate—from the viewpoint of bringing about its golden era—is that the weather usually stays mild throughout the winter. Snow and ice are extremely rare, and rain is uncommon. On most days, you can be quite comfortable outdoors wearing a sweater or jacket, without a topcoat.

Now, the geology, which is a bit more complicated. Aeons ago, the Atlantic Ocean covered all of what is now the low country of the Carolinas (it's called tidewater country in Virginia). There was a great geological upheaval of some kind which caused the sea to retreat nearly seventy miles to the present coastline. The original shoreline, with its sandy bottom and rows of dunes, was left high and dry. This narrow belt of sand hills runs almost as straight as a surveyor's line through the states of the Southeast. Just above it is the fall line, where every river undergoes a sudden sharp drop. Above that is the rocky red clay of the Piedmont region.

Countless centuries of leaf fall from abundant forests have covered the sand hills with a deep mulch, and have converted the soil from infertile sand into a special kind of sandy loam. It absorbs water so quickly that you can take a walk or ride a horse or play golf within an hour after a relatively heavy rain.

Aiken's mild, dry winter climate, and the quick absorption of its sandy loam soil, might never have become the assets they are today were it not for the adventitious circumstance that a frail little girl named Louise Eustis came to Aiken, at the age of six, for a visit with her aunt. "Lulie" Eustis fell in love with the quiet little town—and with horses. Winter after winter she returned to Aiken, where, she had discovered with delight, "you can go riding every day, even in February."

Lulie Eustis grew up and married a wealthy New Yorker named Thomas C. Hitchcock, who owned a stable of race horses and was a member of America's first international polo team. Mr. and Mrs. Hitchcock built a winter home in Aiken and named it Mon Repos. They also acquired thousands of acres of adjacent pine forest, now known as the Hitchcock Woods. Among the towering longleaf pine trees, Lulie Hitchcock laid out riding trails and several steeplechase courses for "drag hunts." (In a drag hunt, the hounds and riders follow, not a live fox, but a scented trail created just before the hunt by dragging a bag of anise over the ground.) Mrs. Hitchcock continued to ride through the woods and take the jumps as gracefully as any teen-aged

51

equestrienne until her death at the age of sixty-eight. In her later days, her eyesight began to fail and she couldn't see the jumps until she was almost upon them. Author Kay Lawrence, in her charming history of Aiken, *Heroes, Horses and High Society*, tells how Mrs. Hitchcock solved this problem without submitting to what she regarded as the indignity of wearing glasses. She saw to it that she was always accompanied on drag hunts by one of her granddaughters. At precisely the right moment, the young escort would shout, "Jump, Gram!" and the gallant lady would send her horse sailing over the five-foot-high barrier of logs in perfect form.

The Hitchcocks became missionaries for Aiken. They were so enthusiastic about it as a heaven for horse lovers they soon persuaded many of their wealthy friends to build homes and stables in Aiken. One of the first to join them was William C. Whitney, a prominent New York banker and sportsman. Whitney built a polo field, one of the first in America. "Whitney Field" remains to this day one of the world's foremost centers of polo playing. Every Sunday afternoon from February until April, high-goal polo is played there. The field has served several times as the site of the annual National Polo Tournament, in which teams from every part of the country compete over a period of about two weeks.

Aiken polo has produced some of the greatest players in the history of the sport, including Thomas Hitchcock, Jr., first American to be designated a ten-goal player, the highest rating possible. Other Aiken polo players who have achieved international fame include Pete Bostwick, Lewis Smith, Alan Corey, Jr., Norty Knox, Devereux Milburn, F. S. von Stade, Raymond Guest, Fred Post, and Billy Post.

Horsemen who came to ride drag hunts in Hitchcock Woods or play polo on Whitney Field soon saw other

52

possibilities in Aiken. They built enormous stables and training tracks, and sent their fledgling horses to Aiken to be prepared for their eventual debuts at the famous racing tracks of the East. Aiken became—and still is—one of America's chief training centers for both thoroughbreds (flat racers and steeplechasers) and standardbreds (harness racing trotters and pacers).

Even to one such as I, who know very little about horses and still less about riding them, Aiken's involvement with the sport of kings is a source of unending fascination. It gives the town color and flavor—especially during the month of March each year. In March, Aiken has three successive Saturdays of racing. First come the famous Aiken Trials, at which horses ready to "graduate" from training run their first competitive races. There are no purses and no pari-mutuel betting, but the trials draw horse lovers from all over America who know that a great many future Kentucky Derby and Belmont winners have won their first races at the Aiken Trials.

The trials are followed a week later by harness races at the Aiken Mile Track. Again, there's no (legal) betting, but the standardbreds on display are among the finest trotters and pacers in the land.

Finally, the season culminates with the Aiken Hunt Meeting, at which jumpers compete in a race sanctioned by the National Steeplechase Association. There are modest purses for some of the races, but the big prizes are the Imperial Cup and the Aiken Cup. One of the highlights of the Aiken Hunt Meeting is a mule race, in which prominent public figures, including governors and congressmen, serve as jockeys. Inducing a mule to move at all is no mean feat, and getting it into a gallop is little short of a miracle. The mule race always creates wild excitement, and large sums are wagered privately and informally on which of the balky animals will meander across the finish line first. There are no photo finishes in the Aiken Mule Derby.

Each of the three-race meets is a great occasion for "tailgate parties." A tailgate party is a special kind of picnic, and Aiken has brought it to a high state of development. Regular racegoers have reserved parking spaces at the rail. (The fees charged for these spaces are donated to local charities such as the hospital building fund.) A group of friends will retain year after year a particular block of adjacent spaces. On race day, on the open tailgates of their wagons and on supplementary picnic tables set up nearby, they spread elaborate picnic lunches. Some of the tables are grandly decorated with flowers and silver candelabra. Potables are provided in great quantity and variety. Bloody Marys and *kir* (dry white wine laced with *crème de cassis*) are among the most popular items dispensed by tailgate bartenders. Few hostesses stoop to picnic fare so mundane as sandwiches. Their menus run instead to such things as London broil, *filet mignon* cooked over portable charcoal grills, chicken Kiev, tossed salads, lavish trays of hors d'oeuvres, homemade cakes, and pecan pies.

Since every racing Saturday is preceded and followed by one or two evenings of cocktail and dinner parties, and since nearly everyone has a houseful of out of town guests, March weekends in Aiken are very jolly if slightly wearing occasions. After the Aiken Hunt, everyone collapses and there is an unwritten law that no one should invite anyone to anything for at least two weeks.

The "horse people," who remain in Aiken from late November until mid-April, thus maintain some of the festivity and glamour of Aiken's heyday. But the golden era of the winter colony was the half century between 1890 and the outbreak of World War II. Since World War II, income taxes have made it virtually impossible for wealthy families to live on the scale that was commonplace in the Aiken winter colony in the days when Aiken at least rivaled and perhaps outdistanced Palm Beach, Newport, Bar Harbor, and Saratoga as a gathering place for the very rich.

In those fabulous days, the Aiken winter colony included, in addition to Hitchcocks, Whitneys, Bostwicks, and Knoxes, such rich and/or famous people as Mrs. C. Oliver Iselin; Mr. and Mrs. Eugene Grace; Mr. and Mrs. W. R. Grace; Mr. and Mrs. Edmund P. Rogers (frequent hosts to the Duke and Duchess of Windsor); Miss Claudia Phelps; Mr. and Mrs. Walter Phelps; Col. Robert R. McCormick, Mrs. David Dows; Mr. and Mrs. F. Ambrose Clark; Mr. and Mrs. James E. Burden; assorted Vanderbilts and Harrimans; and the lovely Lucy Mercer Rutherfurd, whose close friend Franklin D. Roosevelt often visited her Aiken home.

Other frequent visitors were John Jacob Astor; Mr. and Mrs. Winston Churchill; Count Ilia Tolstoi; Josef Hofman; Will Rogers; and Fred Astaire.

At the peak of the season, as many as eight or ten private Pullman cars might be lined up on the sidetrack of Aiken's tiny railroad station. A train called the Aiken Special ran daily from New York. Before a big weekend of racing or polo, it might carry 50 sleeping cars filled with horsemen and horsewomen, and 60 livestock cars filled with horses. It has been alleged that after some particularly lively weekends, the accommodations were reversed for the trip back to New York. But this story probably is apocryphal.

Most of the permanent or year-after-year members of the winter colony built "cottages" in Aiken. They were not marble palaces such as one finds in Newport; Aiken tradition has always frowned on that kind of ostentation. But they were (and are) enormous. For example, the Whitney residence, Joye Cottage (very appropriately located at the corner of Whiskey Road and Easy Street), has ninety rooms.

Many others are almost as large. Most of these huge homes are rambling wooden structures, with cavernous ballrooms, long banquet halls, and enormous numbers of bedrooms to accommodate a constantly ebbing and flowing tide of guests.

Anyone who did not own or rent a cottage, or who was not invited to put up in one as a visitor, found lodging at the Willcox Hotel, a handsome inn of southern Colonial architecture. The Willcox (no longer in operation) provided magnificent food and service at extremely high prices.

Long after the advent of the motor car, Aiken's winter colony got about in horse-drawn carriages and pony carts. On a weekday in January you could find as many as forty such vehicles parked outside Hahn's or Schulhofer's, the stores which purveyed foods and wines for the winter colony's tables.

Each cottage had a large staff of servants, and there was at least one big dinner party every evening during the season. Balls—occasionally costume but usually white tie—were held nearly every Friday and Saturday evening.

On one of these weekends—and this story is *not* apocryphal—a wealthy young banker who loved to play polo came down from New York on the Aiken Special, arriving Friday afternoon. He checked into the Willcox, where he continued the steady absorption of Scotch he had begun on the train.

Late Sunday afternoon one of the impeccable footmen of the Willcox staff gently awakened him and told him he had just an hour to catch the last train that would get him back to New York by Monday afternoon, which was regarded as the deadline for a young gentleman associated with the House of Morgan to return to his office after a weekend trip.

The woozy young man hastily dressed and dashed to the train. Before leaving, he arranged with the hotel to send two dozen roses, a magnum of champagne, and his abject note of apology to the Aiken hostess who had asked him to dine at her home Saturday.

He received within a few days a letter from the Aiken hostess. "Thanks for the flowers and champagne," she said. "But why the apologies? You were the life of the party."

ONE DAY, soon after we moved to Coontail Lagoon, my wife returned from a trip to the grocery store wearing a puzzled expression.

"What's bothering you?" I asked.

"There were two women ahead of me at the checkout counter," she said. "They were talking about something that happened last night at a PTA meeting. I wasn't paying much attention until one of them said, 'Oh, well, it's been that way ever since the town was overrun with bombers.'"

We had received no previous intimation that Aiken was a hotbed of petard-heavers. On the contrary, the few political discussions into which I'd been drawn had left me with a strong impression that if Aiken were overrun with anything, it was Republicans.

I decided Charlotte must have misunderstood the woman at the checkout counter, and put the matter out of mind.

A few days later, however, I encountered at a party a clean-cut young man who informed me, in response to my routine inquiry about his occupation: "I am a bomber."

I looked him up and down quickly, paying particular attention to his pockets. But I saw no telltale bulges that would indicate he was carrying an infernal device. He noticed my scrutiny and seemed amused by it.

"Haven't you heard about us bombers?" he asked.

"Nothing comprehensible. What do you bomb, and why do they let you run around loose?"

"Oh, we don't bomb anybody—directly, at least. People here call us bombers because we work at the Savannah River Plant."

The Savannah River Plant is the biggest thing that has happened to Aiken since the heyday of the winter colony. It is a huge industrial complex in which the U.S. Government, via the Atomic Energy Commission, has invested some three billion dollars since land acquisition and construction got underway in 1950. Today, it is America's chief center of plutonium production.

Plutonium, as you doubtless know, is a man-made fissionable element. It can be and is used for benign purposes as fuel in a nuclear power reactor. But it's best known as the stuff that goes bang in a hydrogen bomb. So it was probably inevitable that the Savannah River Plant would come to be known locally as "the bomb plant," and its five thousand employees (including stenographers who've never been within two miles of a plutonium reactor) as "bombers."

The Du Pont Company, which operates the plant for the government, hired local labor to the fullest possible extent. But so many esoteric skills are needed to operate reactors and their related paraphernalia, Du Pont had to recruit scientists, engineers, and technicians from every part of the country to fill out the staff of the Savannah River plant.

The bomb plant was just the beginning of Aiken's belated industrial revolution. Within a few years, farming, once the county's chief source of livelihood, had become a comparatively rare occupation, primarily attractive to wealthy people in search of a tax shelter. In fields that were planted to cotton and peanuts in my youth now stand handsome factories where Owens-Corning makes Fiberglas, Kimberly-

59

Clark makes Kleenex, Riegel Textiles makes throwaway diapers, and Allied Gulf Nuclear Services (a joint venture of Allied Chemical and Gulf Oil) recycles spent fuel cylinders from nuclear power plants.

Each of these (and many other) industrial plants has brought with it a complement of managerial and technological personnel—highly paid, highly educated people, full of Yankee vigor but very susceptible to Aiken's southern charm. They have invested enormous energy and competence in improving Aiken's schools, churches, and civic organizations, and are apt to be even more zealous than native-born citizens about preserving the atmosphere and traditions of the unique little town they've adopted as home.

As a result, Aiken now has year-round the extraordinarily cosmopolitan flavor it used to take on only in winter, when the "rich Yankees" of the horse set arrived for their annual sojourn.

The establishment at Aiken of a regional campus of the University of South Carolina and the town's growing popularity as a retirement community have further contributed to the heterogeneity of the population. In addition to Yankees, southerners, midwesterners, and westerners, in approximately equal numbers, Aiken now has a leavening of Europeans, Asians, and Latin Americans, and even a few Texans. I doubt if any other small town on earth has such a mixed bag of humanity.

The retirement community centers around a subdivision called Crosland Park, and has brought to Aiken a large contingent of still-sprightly men and women who achieved notable success in business or professional careers.

When the Rt. Rev. John E. Hines was nearing the end of his term as presiding Bishop of the Episcopal Church, he visited Aiken and commented on its spreading fame as a place to retire.

"Tell me," he asked an Aiken resident who was sitting beside him at dinner, "do you have any worn-out old bishops living here?"

The Aiken resident thought for a moment and replied politely:

"No, sir. You'll have that field entirely to yourself."

Conversation at an Aiken dinner party is apt to range all over the world. And it's rare that you don't find someone at the table who has lived in or at least visited whatever far-away place happens to be under discussion.

Any corner of the earth that has been missed is not likely to remain long as *terra incognita*, for travel surpasses even horses and golf as Aiken's favorite sport.

It seems sometimes that our friends are forever leaving on or returning from trips—to Europe, Asia, South America, or around the world. Since every leave-taking and every return calls for celebration, there are a great many parties. If you haven't been told in advance, the first question you ask, upon arriving at a social function, is, "Who's going where?" If your hostess replies, "They're not *going*, dear, they just got back," you still need to know who and where, so you can ask the appropriate questions. When you are unable to obtain any light on these matters before you find yourself in conversation with one who is clearly a recent returner, I have discovered that you usually can muddle through by asking, "How was the food?"

When conversation veers away from geography, it usually turns to culture. I understand from things I've read and heard that this passion for culture is becoming a national phenomenon, but I doubt whether any town of comparable size has such a virulent case as Aiken. Where else would a community of less than twenty thousand persons undertake to supply both talent and patronage for an opera society, a civic ballet, a community playhouse and a symphony orchestra? I must admit the performances are not always up to the standards of the Kennedy Center or the Lincoln Center. But I would remind any carping critic of what Dr. Samuel Johnson said to Boswell about the gait of a dog who had been trained to walk on his hind legs: The remarkable thing is not that it is done *well*, but that it is done at all.

It's hard to say exactly what causes a place to become a haven for artists and writers. Sometimes—as in Greenwich Village or on the Left Bank of Paris many years before they became fashionable—the initial attraction is purely economic: it's a cheap place to live. Scenery and climate—things to paint and plenty of good light to paint in—also may play a major role, as they surely have at Provincetown on Cape Cod, and at Carmel, California, and the adjacent Big Sur country. Sometimes, it seems, it is just a matter of two or three creative people finding themselves in the same place, and establishing an atmosphere that draws other artists or writers. That, in part, may account for the incredible concentration of talent in Florence during the Renaissance.

All three of these factors seem to have been involved in attracting an unusually high percentage of artists, writers, and other creatively talented people to Aiken. The influx of painters and of artists (or craftsmen—I'm never sure which is which) who produce objects of beauty from clay, stone, wood, cloth, rope, and metal has been most conspicuous since the mid-1960's, but I gather it began on a small scale well before that time. In any case, Aiken had become by the 1970's an artists' colony (and on a much more modest scale, a writers' colony) comparable to Carmel or Provincetown.

Most of the creative ferment revolves around the Rose Hill Art Center, a nonprofit institution which is domiciled (rent-free) in the onetime stables and kennels of Miss

Claudia Phelps's handsome estate, Rose Hill. Miss Phelps's niece, Nancy Wilds, one of the few practicing illuminatists in the contemporary world, and Pat Koelker, pretty and talented artist, started the Rose Hill Center on a budget that made a shoestring seem a costly luxury. Now the whole community is behind the center, contributing cash, time, work, and concern to its rapid growth. At one Rose Hill patrons' party (aptly billed "An Evening of Wine and Roses"), I found myself in a convivial group that included the president of a huge corporation, who had written a fat check for the center, and a journeyman electrician who had done all the wiring and forgotten to send a bill. As we talked about the paintings on display (a blessed relief from horses and travel talk), I quickly discovered that both the executive and the electrician were quite knowledgeable about art —and both knew far more about it than I did. It is very difficult in Aiken to maintain your stereotypes about business Babbitts and blue-collar workers.

SOME PEOPLE—a small but blessed minority—seem to mellow as they grow old. Instead of becoming irritable and hypercritical, they develop a gentle tolerance for the foibles and eccentricities of other human beings.

Once in a great while you find a town in which this spirit of tolerance, if not universal, is so widespread that it is the dominant social attitude. Even those who would privately prefer to be harshly judgmental are deterred from publicly voicing their criticisms, because they know that running other people down is the one thing that is *not* tolerated in that community.

San Francisco is such a place, which is one reason it is my favorite big city. I never expected to find the same spirit in any small town, because I was imbued with the myth that small towns are hotbeds of gossip and intolerance.

Perhaps some small towns really are like that. I've never been to Peyton Place and I'll have to take Grace Metalious' word for what it's like. But my wife and I have learned to our delight that Aiken is fully as imperturbable as San Francisco. You may earn its disapproval, if you work at it hard enough, but you cannot shock Aiken.

The extremely wide limits it sets for eccentric conduct were demonstrated by the case of a young person who grew up in Aiken wearing dresses and bearing a girl's name. This person went abroad, returned wearing male attire and announced that she (or should it be he?—pronouns get very difficult in these situations) had undergone a sex-change operation in Sweden and henceforth should be addressed as George. Although George was inclined to discuss his operation in graphic clinical detail at every opportunity, he continued to be accepted in polite society until he started to call on ladies of his acquaintance and insist that they inspect the results of his surgery. This proved to be too much even for Aiken, and George ceased to be invited to parties.

Fortunately, George's conduct eventually came to the attention of a psychiatrist who lives in retirement in Aiken. This compassionate physician helped George complete psychologically the change which had been achieved only physically in Sweden. I am happy to report that George is now well adjusted and a welcome guest at parties.

Aiken society has evolved an extremely useful phrase which enables hostesses to cope with situations such as George's period of exhibitionism without stooping to gossip. When one woman wishes to convey to another that a particular individual has some idiosyncrasy which makes it risky to invite him or her to a party, she simply says that the person in question is "not social."

Since I first encountered this delightful expression, I have heard it employed to describe acute alcoholics, mental defectives, aged recluses, a man who insists on bringing his mistress to parties where he knows his wife will be present, and one hapless fellow who is suspected of doping horses. Only in the latter case did I detect what seemed to be a small note of scorn.

Aiken's distaste for gossip, even about the great and powerful, is most clearly demonstrated, perhaps, by the fact that no one in Aiken will discuss to this day the universally known fact that Franklin D. Roosevelt, while President of the United States, visited frequently at the Aiken home of his very dear friend Mrs. Lucy Mercer Rutherfurd. It was not until years after Roosevelt and Mrs. Rutherfurd died that Jonathan Daniels, a North Carolina newspaperman who had worked on Roosevelt's White House staff, disclosed the visits in a book. Then the whole country went into a tizzy over FDR's "secret romance." Mrs. Eulalie Salley, who had been very close to Mrs. Rutherfurd, succinctly voiced Aiken's view of this belated scandal. When a CBS television interviewer thrust a microphone at her and demanded that she comment on the Roosevelt-Rutherfurd relationship, Mrs. Salley replied with frosty dignity:

"Mr. Daniels is no gentleman."

(Actually, he *is* a gentleman, and a fine one. He simply did not realize that such a hot bit of gossip could have been so utterly repressed for so long a time in such a small town.)

Many great Aiken stories are buried forever, under the seal of the confessional, in the capacious memory of the Rt. Rev. Msgr. George Lewis Smith, a longtime rector of St. Mary Help of Christians, Aiken's large and thriving Catholic parish. Msgr. Smith, himself a great horseman and onetime polo star, served for nearly half a century as unofficial chaplain to both Protestants and Catholics in the winter colony. My wiliest endeavors as a reporter have not succeeded in extracting from him anything he shouldn't reveal, but he did tell me one story, carefully deleting all names and other possible points of identification, that magnificently illustrates Aiken's spirit of live-and-let-live.

Each winter a wealthy man and his wife came to live in their huge, brick-walled "cottage" on Whiskey Road. The gentleman brought along not only his horses but also his mistress. She was stabled separately in a small but comfortable house near South Boundary, about two miles from his home. Each evening after dinner he would bid his wife good evening, explaining that he had a date to play bridge with some male friends. She knew very well he was going to visit his mistress, but always went along with the bridge story without demur.

One cold and rainy night the sportsman did a poor job of tying the reins when he drove his horse and carriage up to the front of his mistress' house. While he was engaged inside, the reins came loose, and the rain-soaked horse trotted home to seek the shelter of his barn.

The wife heard the carriage clattering into the yard, hours ahead of schedule. Looking out, she saw it was empty and surmised what must have happened.

"Would you believe," said Msgr. Smith, "that she awakened a groom and gave him explicit instructions. He was to return the horse and carriage to the house of the mistress, whose address she well knew, tie the reins securely, and slip quietly away. The philandering husband emerged about midnight, found his carriage waiting as usual, and drove home complacently. To his dying day, he never knew what his wife had done to spare him from the embarrassment of having to walk home in the rain."

I believe it, but only because it happened in Aiken.

Birds and animals are greatly cherished in Aiken, and are frequently involved in episodes which demonstrate its unflappability in the presence of circumstances or behavior that might be regarded in other places as somewhat eccentric.

One Sunday, Charlotte and I were walking up the gravel driveway toward St. Thaddeus Episcopal church, just in time for the eleven o'clock service. Ahead of us walked two ladies. I recognized one as a member of the congregation. The other apparently was an out-of-town visitor.

Nearing the entrance, the visitor chanced to look up into the overhanging branches of a massive magnolia tree.

"My God!" she cried, in what I feel sure was an impromptu prayer. "Look at that big bird!"

"That's no bird," said her hostess soothingly. "That's St. Francis."

I could not discern that this reply was immediately clarifying or comforting to the visitor. If anything, she seemed more thunderstruck than before.

"St. Francis," the hostess went on after a very long moment, "is the church chicken."

She did not volunteer further explanation and the visitor, understandably wary of asking any more questions, tottered on into church, slowly shaking her head.

St. Francis has been around our church so long it just doesn't occur to members of the congregation that her presence may come as a shock to strangers.

No one seems able to recall just when she joined St. Thaddeus. The gardener, whom I queried on the matter, told me that "she just walked in and took up here several years ago."

The rector, the Rev. Howard Hickey, made some remark to the effect that he felt like St. Francis, who preached the gospel to birds and animals. So, naturally, everyone started calling our chicken St. Francis.

Cracked corn is provided regularly in the church budget to keep St. Francis in provender. Her housing presents no problem, since she has elected to roost in the magnolia tree.

On very cold mornings St. Francis tends to remain in the tree huddled against the chill. But on sunny days she struts back and forth along the gravel walk, greeting parishioners as they arrive and depart.

She is a very dignified chicken, but I have been unable to ascertain anything about her background or lineage.

"Is she a Rhode Island Red?" I asked a lady who takes an active part in parish affairs and generally can be relied upon to know everything about everyone.

"Oh, I don't think so," she replied. "She's just a chicken chicken."

Father Hickey is as deeply involved in Aiken's life as Msgr. Smith. Every Thanksgiving Day, when Msgr. Smith blesses the hounds for the season's first hunt in Hitchcock Woods, Father Hickey stands in the background saying, as he puts it, "a silent prayer for the fox."

One day some children, who had grown up in St. Thaddeus and knew Father Hickey's love of animals, came to him in tears to report that their dog was dying.

"The vet says he can't do a thing for him," sobbed one little girl. "Would you come over and say a prayer for him?"

Howard Hickey gravely donned his clerical vestments and followed the children to their home. He finally found in the Book of Common Prayer ("If you look long enough, you can find *anything* in there") a collect which seemed appropriate to the occasion. He said the prayer, patted the sick dog on the head, and returned to the church.

"You know," he told me with a half-serious grin, "that dog got well and is still trotting around town. Every time I see him with those children, I have to be careful to keep an absolutely matter-of-fact look on my face. I wouldn't want them to think I was surprised."

"IT'S LIKE LOOKING at Pompeii," my wife said in a stunned whisper.

No, I thought. It's even worse than that. Pompeii at least has ruins that show where a town stood before it got in the way of a volcano nearly two thousand years ago.

There are not even ruins to mark where my hometown, Ellenton, stood before it got in the way of a government project in 1950. The project was, and is, the Savannah River plant of the U.S. Atomic Energy Commission. It has cost the taxpayers more than three billion dollars to date. It is the world's largest and most highly automated factory. It is the principal U.S. facility for production of plutonium, the essential ingredient of hydrogen bombs and nuclear power plants.

The engineers of the Atomic Energy Commission conducted a year-long search of all parts of America to find the most suitable site for this gigantic manufacturing complex, which dwarfs even Ford's River Rouge plant. They settled on Ellenton and its environs for two principal reasons. First, the site adjoined the Savannah River, from which millions of gallons of water could be drawn daily through pipes seven feet in diameter to cool the plant's widely dispersed reactors. Second, Ellenton and the surrounding farm country were, by the cold-blooded calculations of engineers, "sparsely populated."

Well, I suppose they were. But within the 250,000 acres which the Atomic Energy Commission seized—and that is the precise legal term—lived some six thousand human beings, all of whom had deep roots in the sandy loam of western Carolina. Most of them had spent their entire lives in Ellenton. Many operated farms or businesses that had been in the same family for seven or eight generations. There was an intricate network of human ties: family relationships, blood kinships, friendships—in short, a deep sense of community. All of this was destroyed and all of the people were cruelly uprooted because the engineers decided this was where they wanted to build that plutonium plant.

Years afterward an Atomic Energy Commission official, who had been involved in the original land seizure, told me privately that it would have been possible to let Ellenton stay in existence. None of the reactors or other facilities of the plant are located within the area where the town used to stand.

"But it would have been administratively inconvenient," he said. "We felt it would be better just to get those people out of there."

I don't know whether he didn't realize, or just didn't care, that "those people" included my father and mother, scores of aunts, uncles and cousins, and hundreds of friends of my childhood.

They didn't protest very much about being uprooted, although it distressed nearly all of them greatly. The patriotism of the Deep South is an instinctive thing. These people had given their sons when their country said it needed them to fight in wars, and they certainly would not balk at giving up their homes when their country said it needed them to prepare for possible future war.

The Government promised to pay them well for their property. But it lied. The first few settlement checks were fairly generous. But then *Life* magazine got in the act, publishing a full-page, posed picture of an overalled black farmer, grinning widely as he looked at what *Life* called his unexpectedly large check. The day the magazine came out, big bureaucratic wheels in Washington telephoned the land acquisition staff in South Carolina with an urgent warning: Cut those settlements drastically or we'll be getting static from Congress.

Thereafter, the people—who soon began calling themselves, with grim humor, "the first DP's of World War III"—learned that when the Government wants your land, it doesn't have to negotiate the price with you. It just seizes the property and deposits to your credit a sum which it has unilaterally determined to be a "fair" price. If you feel the price is far below the real value of the property, as most of the DP's did, you can go into federal court and sue the Government for additional compensation. But that takes a long time, and most of the dispossessed families, having no other resources, could not afford to wait the outcome of such a suit. So they took the settlement their government offered them, never suspecting it was deliberately kept artificially low to please economy-minded congressmen and Atomic Energy Commission officials in Washington.

Those who did elect to go to court invariably got substantially larger sums than they were originally offered, but legal costs ate up much of the additional payment. One of the Aiken lawyers who earned huge fees handling seizure cases was Strom Thurmond. His fees from my family alone were sufficient to finance his successful campaign for election to the U.S. Senate, a circumstance that has always made me feel a vague personal responsibility for his subsequent political career.

The worst aspect of the niggardly settlements, I think, was the unshakable conviction of persons outside the condemned area—a conviction that persists in Aiken to this day—that the DP's "got rich" off the Government's checks. It is bad enough to be cheated by your government; it rubs salt in the wound to have others think you the recipient of open-handed largesse.

All of this happened more than twenty years ago, and if I still sound bitter about it (as I am), it is due to the fact that only since my return to Aiken County have I really known the true facts. On the twentieth anniversary of the seizure announcement, the Atomic Energy Commission *boasted* in a publicity release that *timber* which had been cut from, or was still standing on, the 250,000 acres seized in 1950 was worth more than the entire price paid by the Government for buildings, farms, business firms, and all the other assets, besides timberlands, which were seized.

This extraordinary boast caused me to seek out a retired official who had played a key role in the land seizure. He told me:

"I always was and still am deeply ashamed of the prices we paid those folks. We knew we were robbing them, but we had explicit orders from Washington to reduce settlement offers drastically. It was that *Life* picture that did it."

Charlotte and I were given permission to revisit the site of Ellenton with a formidable escort of Atomic Energy Commission employees. One member of the party, fortunately, was a civil engineer. With the aid of a map and transit, he was able to tell me exactly where my home had been, where my father's store had stood, where the railroad station was, where I went to school, the site of the cemetery from which the bodies of my ancestors were removed for reburial outside the "bomb plant" area.

Without the help of the engineer, we could not have

identified any of these places, for the Atomic Energy Commission, evidently desiring to leave no visible evidence of its act of "village-cide," has carefully destroyed everything that once stood in Ellenton, including the foundations of buildings. There is nothing, literally nothing, but a rank growth of weeds, trees, and once lovingly cultivated shrubbery that has gone wild.

The worst emotional shock came when we went down to the riverbank, at a point where my family had owned a three-thousand-acre tract of virgin cypress swamp, untouched by man since it came to one of my ancestors by royal grant in 1734. You know how I feel about swamps. There are precious few large expanses of cypress swamp left in America. This had been one of the largest and loveliest. But the Savannah River plant has found it convenient— that seems to be their ultimate test of everything—to use the swamp as a "cooling basin" for the very hot water that comes out of the reactors. The swamp today is a graveyard of dead cypress trees, their leafless hulks still rising 150 feet from the water, in mute protest against one of the crudest rapes of nature ever perpetrated by our government.

The crowning irony—the Atomic Energy Commission seems to have a knack for irony—was the announcement in 1972 that the Savannah River plant was being declared an "ecological laboratory" where scientists could make environmental studies. Conservation groups and editorial writers praised the commission profusely for this noble gesture. What no one thought to point out was that the plant area is of interest to ecologists partly because it is a classic example of the destructive impact of a massive industrial operation on a hitherto-unspoiled natural environment.

I am told by Atomic Energy Commission officials that plutonium will be the nation's chief source of energy by the end of this century, and I think that probably is true. If so, my old hometown will be a national resource comparable to the oil fields of Texas and Oklahoma or the coal mines of Pennsylvania and West Virginia. I suppose that thought should make me feel proud. But, quite frankly, I wish they had built the damned plant somewhere else.

While it lasted, which was more than two hundred years, Ellenton was a wonderful place to live. It was very much like one of the small river port towns on the Mississippi that have been so perfectly described by Mark Twain.

The center of town, both geographically and in terms of activity, was a general store built by my grandfather and known to everyone as The Long Store. It came by this appellation honestly, since it was a frame building about 50 feet in width and 210 feet long.

By the front door was the drug and cosmetic counter, and the department where "notions" (thread, ribbons, and the like) were displayed. Next came a large section devoted to "dry goods"—a category that included everything from cloth-by-the-yard to ready-made dresses, shirts, overalls, and other haberdashery. Adjacent to the dry goods section were the shoe department and the hat shelves.

Beyond this was a sort of no-man's-land—my grandfather evidently felt some separation was in order—before you entered the grocery department. I worked in the grocery department as a clerk every Saturday between my eighth birthday, when I was adjudged old enough to make change accurately, and my seventeenth year, when I left for college. My employment as a grocery clerk coincided with the worst years of the great depression of the 1930's, and I still remember some of the prices: salmon, ten cents a can; fatback, four cents a pound; frankfurters, nineteen cents a pound; flour, seventy-nine cents for a twenty-four-pound bag; rice, five cents a pound; syrup, twenty-nine cents a gallon (if you brought your own jug, to be filled from a giant oak cask).

I need hardly tell you that it is a trauma for me to accompany my wife into a grocery store today. It is a trauma for her too, as I am apt at any moment to stagger back from a price tag and cry aloud in horror.

Beyond the grocery department were segments of the Long Store devoted to hardware, tools, farm implements, fertilizer, and livestock feeds. Contrary to legend, we did not sell caskets in the Long Store. They were sold discreetly from a small, separate building to the rear.

Farm families, who comprised the bulk of the Ellenton area's population, came to the Long Store every Saturday to do their week's shopping. In my youth, the majority came in mule-drawn wagons. To accommodate them, my grandfather had erected hundreds of hitching posts on a large grassy plot adjacent to the store. Years later I returned from college one spring to find the hitching posts gone and the grass replaced by macadam. The wagon field had become a parking lot for cars and pickup trucks. I felt at the time that this was a sign of progress. Now I'm not so sure. Or maybe what I really doubt is whether "progress" is so desirable.

At the very back of the Long Store, commanding a view of its entire length, was the office, which my father occupied after my grandfather's death in 1930. It was known by everyone in Ellenton as "the Bull Pen." The origin of the name is obscure, but I think we all sensed that it was entirely appropriate that Mike Cassels' sanctum sanctorum should be designated by some such robust term.

My father ruled a large part of the economic life of the Ellenton area. In addition to operating the Long Store, we farmed twelve thousand acres of plantation and operated a bank, a chicken farm, a dairy, a canning factory, a telephone company, an electric power company, and a large lumber mill. (The latter was an especial delight of my youth, since

76

it had its own railroad and a little steam engine to haul logs out of the swamp. I was occasionally allowed to "assist" the engineer of this logging train, whom I fondly remember as a man of almost unlimited patience.)

Although his rule was virtually absolute within his realm, "Mr. Mike" was one of the most benevolent despots imaginable. He "carried" hundreds of farm families through the worst times of the depression, by allowing them to buy "on credit" the food, fertilizer, clothing, and other necessities for which they had no money to pay. These "debts" were quietly written off so that pride was preserved. Cotton was bringing five cents a pound in that period, and there was just no way a farmer could make ends meet.

I remember a conversation my father had one Saturday evening with a much-respected black farmer. The farmer described in detail his economic situation, and said he had about despaired of making a living from farming.

"What are you going to do?" my father asked.

The gray-haired farmer drew himself up with dignity and replied:

"Well, Mr. Mike, I've preached before and I'm not too proud to do it again."

I tell this story every time I am invited to address a group of clergymen. None of them has ever found it funny. But it helps to hold down speaking invitations.

It was my father who taught me, during those depression years when I worked for him in his store, that there is almost no human situation which cannot be made more tolerable by a sense of humor. This was one reason he had such a deep rapport with black people, who were a majority of the population of the Ellenton area. Blacks have had so much to endure that they have learned to laugh in the teeth of adversity, and my father laughed with them. Looking back now, I can see what a crushing burden of worry and responsibility he bore, but I remember him primarily as a merry man who loved all kinds and conditions of people, and who relished the making and telling of good jokes.

His closest friend, outside the family, was Paul Culbreath, a physician who embodied, in actual fact, all of the goodness and self-giving generosity that legend attributes to old-time country doctors. Dr. Culbreath also was an avid practical joker. Knowing my father's squeamishness about such things, Dr. Culbreath came into the Long Store one morning and announced cheerfully:

"Mike, I'm going out to the country to amputate a man's leg, and I'm going to bring it back to you as a souvenir."

Two hours later the doctor walked the full length of the Long Store, swinging a gunny sack which contained some fairly heavy object. My father watched his progress toward the Bull Pen in horror. When Dr. Culbreath unceremoniously dropped the sack on his desk, my father didn't pause to examine it: he fled the Bull Pen.

Dr. Culbreath finally persuaded him to return and see what the gunny sack actually contained. It was a limb all right—from a tree.

On the side of the Long Store opposite the mule park there was a fenced enclosure that included an outdoor toilet, better known in that time and place as a privy. This small structure played a part in one of the most embarrassing episodes of my youth. My father had assigned me to clean some rusty plowshares with a highly flammable solvent resembling kerosene. After I had completed the job, I cast about for a safe place to pour the leftover fluid, and decided to dump it into the privy.

A short time later, unfortunately, a distinguished male citizen of Ellenton, finding himself *in extremis* while visiting the Long Store, repaired to the facility in the side yard. He smoked a cigarette while sitting on the privy and, before arising, dropped the burning butt into the hole upon which he sat. There was a great whoosh of flame and smoke as the solvent ignited. The gentleman ran into the Long Store with his pants down, his dignity shattered, and his buttocks badly scorched. Knowing my father's acute sense of the ridiculous, I am sure he was amused, but he knew better than to let it show. To salve the feelings of the very angry victim, he gave me a royal bawling-out for dumping flammable fluid into the privy. At the end of his sharp lecture, when he was sure no one else could see his face, he winked.

For more years than I can remember, my father served as Ellenton's mayor and magistrate. These offices made it necessary for him to serve as judge in all criminal cases which were considered insufficiently serious to be referred to the court at the county seat for jury trial. He held court every Monday night from a wooden bench in front of the Long Store. Large crowds attended these sessions, which usually provided the town with abundant conversational material for the coming week. The chief of police (in fact, he was the entire police force), Mr. Dixie Dunbar, would present each defendant, outline the charges against him, and call forward the alleged victim of the crime and any other possible witnesses. My father conducted court with great informality. He usually began by asking the plaintiff to tell his version. Then he would hear the defendant's version. Finally, other witnesses would be asked for their testimony. My father usually interrogated each witness rather carefully to ascertain whether he might have a bias for or against either party. Mr. Dunbar introduced any police evidence, such as a confiscated weapon, that might have bearing on the case.

If the guilt of the accused seemed to be clearly established, my father would proceed immediately to the imposition of the sentence, which usually consisted of a period of service on the county's road gang. He did not really like sending men to the road gang, where they were poorly fed and housed and subjected to extremely hard work, so his sentences rarely exceeded three months, even for assault with a deadly weapon, which was a fairly commonplace crime in Ellenton, especially when knife fights erupted in jukebox joints on rowdy Saturday nights.

If there was doubt in my father's mind about the guilt or innocence of the accused, or if there seemed to be extenuating circumstances, he would call upon the assembled crowd for an expression of sentiment. Thus the defendant received what amounted to jury by trial by town meeting.

It was a rough-hewn kind of justice and probably violated innumerable statutes. But the people of Ellenton approved of it because they had complete confidence in "Mr. Mike's" fairness. I believe their confidence was justified. I sat by my father through many a court session, and it seems to me, as I recall those always-fascinating evenings, that he came much closer to dispensing genuine justice than modern courts with all of their purported legal safeguards of defendants' rights.

Dixie Land, Where I Was Born In

From Alexis de Tocqueville onward, visitors to the southern tier of American states have sensed they are somehow different from the rest of the country. The South has a distinctive history—it is, for example, the only part of America that has experienced being on the losing side of a war. This history, along with such factors as climate and economic conditions, has created a peculiarly southern subculture that is expressed in many ways, ranging from particular food preferences to a special manner of speaking.

Rediscovering this "southern way of life" has been one of the principal joys of my return from long exile in the urban North. Some things have changed, of course. Increasing industrialization of a region that was, in my youth, predominantly agricultural has had pervasive effect. So has television, which seems to have an unfortunate homogenizing influence on all American life, toning down regional and ethnic distinctions that have long enriched it.

Despite these erosions, I am pleased to find that the South continues to be not quite like any other place on earth. It still has plenty of regional idiosyncrasies. However, they are not necessarily the ones you read about or see in films. Indeed, the true distinctiveness of the South is often obscured by a mass of myth and legend that has little basis in fact.

Let's consider, as a case in point, southern food and drink.

I shudder to think of the impression of southern cooking that must be gained by millions of tourists who pour through the South every year. Unless they happen to be invited into private homes of southern friends, their exposure to southern cuisine takes place entirely in restaurants, hotel coffee shops or, worst of all, the quick-food places which have sprouted along all U.S. highways like toadstools. (I refrain from using the more familiar metaphor because mushrooms may provide edible food.) I regret to say the South today is infested with the same chains of fast-food dispensaries that pollute the neon strips of your own town—and a franchised hamburger tastes the same in Charleston as it does in Poughkeepsie.

There are a few fine restaurants—such as Henry's in Charleston, the Pirate's House in Savannah, the Town Tavern in Augusta—where authentic regional dishes are properly prepared. But the majority of restaurants and coffee shops in the South seem to be trying—often quite ineptly —to ape the menus and food preparation techniques of big city restaurants in the North. This unhappy emulation may extend to using the same kinds of frozen vegetables and the same methods of watering mashed potatoes.

If you have the opportunity to dine in a private home, you may encounter, even there, a housewife who serves peas from a can or biscuits from a cardboard container. She is not necessarily lazy or stupid: she may be trying to let you know that we southerners aren't hicks: we now use all those exotic Yankee foods which you find on the convience food counters of chain groceries. Heaven forgive her; and heaven help her guests.

Should you be so fortunate as to dine at the table of a

84

cook who still prepares southern food as it always has been and always should be prepared, you will find it is indeed distinctive—and magnificent.

One of its principal adornments is fried chicken. I know this sacred term has been profaned by indiscriminate application to the products of some roadside eating places, but I am talking here about the real thing. Genuine southern fried chicken comes to the table crisp and brown—the result of rapid cooking in *very hot* fat.

In the matter of cuisine, I am a passionate appreciator rather than a skilled producer, so I shall not attempt to tell you how to fry chicken properly. I gather it has something to do with choosing tender young fowls, severing them into pieces whose shape and nomenclature are dictated as much by tradition as by the inherent geography of a chicken, and shaking these pieces in a paper bag with flour, salt, pepper, and a bit of cornmeal to add crunchiness. The breaded parts are then carefully immersed in a skillet filled about one inch deep with a cooking oil or fat, which should be, as mentioned previously, smoking hot.

Maybe Colonel Sanders does it this way too—I've never ventured into one of his ubiquitous kitchens—but believe me, it comes out different.

Another great southern dish that has been brought into disrepute by abominable imitations is barbecued pork.

Real southern barbecue takes about twenty-four hours to prepare. Each year, our good neighbor at Coontail Lagoon, Dave Wood, barbecues a homegrown pig to provide a feast for his family and friends on the Fourth of July. Here is how he goes about it:

The pig is slaughtered, its head and feet are removed, and the carcass is hung from the limb of a tree for draining and cleaning. Hot water from a cast-iron outdoor cooking pot is applied to soften the bristles, which then are removed with a straight razor. The first time my Yankee wife witnessed this ritual, she came tearing home to report breathlessly to me, "Dave is *shaving* the pig!" And that, odd as it may sound, is precisely what he was doing.

The bald pink carcass is then spitted on long steel rods, which run vertically along each side of the backbone and horizontally across the front and hind legs. These spits are placed on a low masonry wall that surrounds a rectangular "barbecue pit" about two feet deep. The pit is filled with hickory or oak wood that has been burning slowly for many hours until it has become a mass of white-ashed coals emitting a low but steady heat.

Dave lets the pig roast over this slow fire for about twenty hours, basting it periodically with a mixture of water, vinegar, salt, and black pepper. (The use of barbecue sauces containing tomato catsup, mustard, onions, cayenne, or other seasonings is regarded by purists with utter contempt.)

About once an hour, the spits are lifted and the pig is turned so the other side can cook for a while. Quite a lot of assistants are required for a barbecuing: some to help turn the pig, others to maintain the fuel supply of the roaring bonfire from which the "'cue-master" occasionally gathers a shovelful of burned-down wood coals to replenish the pit.

Since barbecuing is an all-night process involving a whole group of men, it inevitably becomes a social occasion at which beverages of various types are consumed in considerable quantity. Around the fire, tales are told, and someone may strum a guitar. By dawn the smells emanating from the barbecue pit become almost unendurably tantalizing. But Dave will not be hurried by the watering of mouths. The slow cooking continues until the unpredictable moment when he finally determines, by some mystical method I have never been able to fathom, that "the pig's ready."

Pork also plays a key role in what is perhaps the South's

greatest contribution to culinary art: the cooking of vegetables. The first requirement is that the vegetables be fresh from the garden: not a difficult stipulation to meet in small towns where every family has its own garden, or even in larger cities, which invariably have public markets to which farm wives come daily with freshly picked produce.

Insistence on freshness in vegetables is not, of course, distinctively southern. French cooks were being adamant about it centuries before America was settled. The American South's special contribution to vegetable cookery is the discovery that almost any vegetable tastes better if boiled with hunks of salt fat pork. This is known as "fatback," a term which is a bit misleading, inasmuch as the pork comes from the belly rather than the back of a pig.

Fatback is especially prized for adding flavor to nourishing but unappetizing "greens" such as cabbage, collards, and turnip tops. It also does wonders for string beans, peas, and other legumes.

One of my own favorite southern vegetables is rutabaga, a root somewhat larger than a turnip. Unlike turnips, which are apt to be bitter, rutabagas have a delicate, sweet taste. They emerge from boiling a light orange color.

Another orange-colored root that is a classic ingredient of the southern diet is the sweet potato. Sweet potatoes can be candied, brandied, baked and buttered, made into pies, or dressed up with raisins and nuts. I once had an unforgettable dish, prepared by a Virginia lady, in which mashed sweet potatoes were heavily flavored with bourbon. With the exception of that memorable concoction, I personally have never cared much for sweet potatoes, but most southerners do, and they certainly belong in any litany of southern vegetables. So do asparagus, yellow crookneck squash, black-eyed peas, corn (on the cob, in kernels, or made into fritters or soufflé-like pies), and, above all, butterbeans. What we refer to as butterbeans are baby limas, picked and cooked while very immature and succulent.

Southern families do not eat Irish potatoes as often as do people in other parts of the country. In fact, the only traditional Irish potato dish of the South is prepared by boiling tiny new potatoes, dug in the early days of the season when they are still far from fully grown. They are best, I think, cooked in their pink skins.

Fried, mashed, and baked potatoes occupy a prominent a role in the diets of other Americans, but southerners take their starch in the form of rice, grits, biscuits, and corn bread. South Carolina may be rice-oriented to an unusual degree because rice was one of our main crops for more than a century. I cannot recall a single day during my childhood when we did not have a heaping bowl of white rice on the table at the midday meal (called dinner) and again at the evening meal (supper). Rice by itself is rather blah. You need to top it with something flavorful—for example, thick, white chicken gravy, or butterbeans.

For breakfast, southerners eat grits. I cannot understand why Yankees make such heavy weather over grits. It is nothing more or less than dried corn, ground somewhat more coarsely than cornmeal. It is easy to cook: you simply boil it until it is tender and relatively dry. It is eaten with ham gravy if that delectable substance is available, otherwise with butter—never with milk and sugar.

I won't attempt to tell you how to cook southern-style biscuits and corn bread, for two reasons: (1) I don't really know how; and (2) this isn't a recipe book anyway. I will tell you there are several subtle variations of each. All of them are delicious, nourishing, and—regrettably—fattening.

Fruits widely favored among southerners include peaches, cantaloupes, watermelons, plums, and apples, all of which taste best when they are tree- or vine-ripened in your own yard, or in the garden of a farmer who brings them to market fresh each morning.

In the dessert category, perhaps the most distinctive southern dish is pecan pie, a hugely calorific concoction of pastry, corn syrup, and pecans. The runner-up position might go to fruit cakes, usually prepared for Thanksgiving and Christmas, also enormously rich in calories, and always much improved by several weeks of soaking in a mixture of brandy, rum, and bourbon.

Now let me get in a few licks about alleged "favorite dishes" of the South whose popularity is, in my opinion, largely legendary. Heading this infamous list are chitterlings, pronounced "chitlins." These are pig's intestines that have been cleaned as well as possible, which, unfortunately, is not very well. They smell terrible during and after cooking, and it takes a strong stomach to stay in the same house or even the same block with a dish of chitlins. I loathe chitlins, and I suspect many other southerners do —except when they are making a supreme sacrifice to live up to what has been touted for generations as a dear old southern tradition.

Catfish stew also is much overrated as a southern delicacy. It is a kind of chowder made from channel catfish, onions, potatoes, and seasonings. Cooked by a riverbank and amply accompanied by potables, it is edible, which is about all I can say for it. The truly great southern fish dishes are pan-fried bass and bream from fresh water, and shrimp, crab, snapper, flounder, and pompano from salt water.

The principal nonalcoholic beverages of the South are iced tea and Coca-Cola. I do not hesitate to use the brand name, because Coca-Cola was born in the South (at Atlanta) and continues to be regarded by many southerners as the only respectable soft drink to serve to guests. Incidentally, in the South, a Coca-Cola is called "a dope" rather than "a Coke." Many southerners drink Coca-Cola instead of coffee for breakfast, especially in hot weather.

An apparently indestructible myth depicts the mint julep as the South's favorite alcoholic beverage. My only comment on this is that I never saw or tasted a mint julep until I was in my late twenties, when I ordered one at the Brown Hotel in Louisville, Kentucky. The bartender asked me where I came from, and I told him South Carolina.

"Then why are you drinking this stuff?" he asked.

"I just wanted to try it because I've heard so much about its being *the* southern drink," I said. "I thought you people here in Kentucky really lapped it up."

"Naw," he said. "We mostly sell mint juleps to Yankees who come here for the Derby."

The *real* southern tipple was in the past, and to a large extent still is, bourbon and water. *Not*, please, "bourbon and branch water." I don't know who invented that infamous expression, but I do know one Aiken host who has curtailed its use in his house. He keeps handy a pitcher of real branch water—muddy, with a few insects floating on top—and makes a conspicuous business of pouring it into the drink of any guest who asks for "bourbon and branch water."

"Moonshine whiskey," or as it's sometimes referred to in print, "corn likker," still is made in some backwoods areas of the South. Its sole virtue is that, being untaxed, it is relatively cheap. No man who can afford legally distilled whiskey will ever drink moonshine. It is like pouring acid down your throat. Sometimes, when an old automobile radiator has been used as a cooling coil, it will give you a fatal case of lead poisoning.

The only significant rival to legal bourbon as a potable favored by southerners is Scotch whiskey. In my youth very

90

few southerners drank Scotch. Today, for a southern cocktail party, an experienced host will lay in as much Scotch
as bourbon.

Southern drinking is complicated by the fact that most
southerners are Baptists or Methodists, whose churches officially regard consumption of alcohol as sinful. This teaching is obeyed by Baptists and Methodists about as rigorously as the pope's proscription of birth control is obeyed
by Catholics, which is to say, not very rigorously at all.
Southern Presbyterians are ambivalent about drinking.
They do it but do not approve of it. The only southern
Protestants who can drink in public with a clear conscience
are Episcopalians. But a friend of mine thinks things are
loosening up. "The other day," he said, "I saw two Baptists meet in a liquor store, and *they spoke to each other!*"

My FIRST OPPORTUNITY to see the South as others see it came when I "went north to school" (as my father put it) at Duke University in North Carolina. Most of my fraternity brothers were from Illinois, New York, and Pennsylvania. Even though they were attending a southern university (and having their education subsidized by a southern tobacco millionaire), they displayed a sovereign scorn for everything southern, especially our "peculiar" speech habits.

Fresh from a very small town, and painfully cognizant of my lack of sophistication, I dared not dispute these worldly and self-confident youths who had grown up in or near big cities of the East and Midwest.

Timidly I accepted their supreme assurance that their clichés were the only smart ones, their pronunciations the only correct ones, and their mannerisms the only "smooth" ones. To avoid being thought gauche or provincial, I worked hard at eliminating any external manifestation of my southern origin. By the time I was a senior, I had so thoroughly expunged any trace of a southern accent that new acquaintances would express surprise to learn I had grown up on a South Carolina plantation. I daresay my trips home must have been even more painful to my family than the usual collegiate visitation, but they suffered their fool, if not gladly, at least without open complaint. Despite my assiduous efforts at "desouthernizing" myself, I learned—and now thank God for the fact—that one does not so easily exterminate from the inner man the effects of eight generations of southern ancestry. At heart, I remained a southerner during all my years of exile among the northern tribes.

Since I have come home I have reverted quite naturally to southern ways of speaking and behaving. Because this recycle of personality is comparatively new, I can still observe with some detachment the ways in which southern speech and behavior are distinctive.

Let's begin by shooting down a few canards.

Many residents of the North seem to have the idea that the principal hallmark of southern speech is the phrase "you-all." The word is "yawl." Far from being a quaint provincialism, it is a most useful southern contribution to the English language, which suffers acutely from lack of a second person plural pronoun. Failure to distinguish clearly between "you," singular, and "you," plural, has caused incalculable confusion and no little mischief over the centuries. So southerners wisely remedied this awkward situation by providing a plural form for the second person pronoun. In southern conversation, "yawl" is used when—and only when—it is desirable, for the sake of clarity, to stress the plurality of an invitation, welcome, accusation, or other statement addressed to all who may hear or read it. When a single person is being addressed, a southerner says "you" just like anyone else.

The "southern drawl" also has been subjected to an inordinate amount of inaccurate comment. There are a few southerners who draw out their words at such a leisurely pace that one feels a great desire to stab them in the gluteus maximus with a hot needle to hasten the completion of a sentence. But this exaggerated kind of drawl is encountered mainly among women who think it is a sign of gentility, which it certainly is not.

It is a fact that nearly all southerners (there are some conspicuous exceptions) tend to speak more slowly than, say, a person raised in Brooklyn or the Bronx. And there is a characteristic tendency to soften the hard edges of words, for example by dropping a final "g." Participially speaking, you may find a southerner sittin', talkin', eatin', thinkin', or sleepin', but unless he is making a special effort to communicate with Yankees in their own tongue, he will never pronounce an "ing" word with a guttural consonant at the end.

Next to a terminal "g," the consonant most frequently dispensed with in southern enunciation is an internal "l." Its elimination is particularly noticeable, to an unattuned ear, in the standard southern pronunciation of "help." It is "hep." If a southerner tells you he'll be "glad to hep you," he is not offering to render you au courant but simply to provide succor or assistance. (That he often extends this offer of "hep" to total strangers, and sincerely means it, is another southern trait that is noteworthy, although not directly relevant to the present discussion of speech habits.)

A southerner who feels compelled to decline a request or invitation will tell you, with fervent regret, that he simply "cain't" do what you've asked. The substitution of a long "a" for a short "a" in the abbreviation of "cannot" is an infallible test of southern speech—and the one habit I never managed fully to shake during my absence from the South.

One conspicuous characteristic of southern speech which has nothing to do with pronunciation is an affinity for hyperbole. When a southerner tells a story—and many southerners are excellent raconteurs—he never hesitates to improve upon the truth with a little judicious exaggeration or outright invention. His southern listeners expect this and make the necessary discounts in formulating their impressions of what actually happened. But this inborn disposition to make every tale entertaining, even at the cost of making it tall, can be quite baffling to nonsoutherners. Nearly two decades after my father's death, I am still explaining to the "Yankee daughter-in-law" whom he loved so dearly that some of his great stories should not be regarded as authentic family history.

The southern talent for overstatement is especially conspicuous in social relations. If a southern hostess tells you her life will be devastated and her social career will lie about her in ruins if you don't come to dinner next Tuesday, you may decline if you wish, without fear that she will hang herself in the basement. She'll simply move on to the next name on her list—and go through the same routine. Southern hospitality is real, but it is never quite as urgent as polite convention dictates that it be made to sound.

I could ramble on about southern idiosyncrasies of language, but I am fearful of telling you more about penguins than you really want to know. So I will mention only one more: the universal use of "sir" and "ma'am." There is no mystery about the origin of this habit. Every southern child is taught, from the moment he is able to speak, that adult males should be addressed as "sir" and adult females as "ma'am" (the latter obviously being a contraction of "madam").

In my youth, white children were told to withhold these courteous addresses from black adults. But I am happy to report this particular piece of racism has gone with the wind. The fact that black men and women are routinely addressed by whites as "sir" or "ma'am" is a striking symbol of the dramatic changes that have occurred in southern race relations, which I'll discuss at greater length in the next chapter.

People who have been raised in the South continue all their lives to say "sir" or "ma'am" not only to elders but also to any person with whom they are not on a basis of intimate, first-name familiarity. You also say "yes, sir"; "no, sir"; "yes, ma'am"; and "no, ma'am" to parents, grandparents, aunts, and uncles. The omission of "sir" or "ma'am," especially in addressing an older person, is universally regarded as rude and disrespectful.

I think this custom, which happily shows no signs of waning, is a clue to one of the dominant traits of southern character. Southerners value courtesy very highly. They regard it—rightly, I believe—as an essential lubricant of human relationships. During my years in New York and Washington, I often found myself thinking how much more pleasant things would be, how much tension and abrasiveness might be eliminated from interpersonal and intergroup contacts, if people would only say "please," "thank you," and "I beg your pardon," as southerners do instantly and automatically in every appropriate situation.

It is well that formal courtesy is so deeply ingrained in southern manners, for it helps to moderate another southern characteristic which has been commented upon by every perceptive observer since W. J. Cash wrote his classic diagnosis of *The Mind of the South*.

This southern trait, which also, unfortunately, shows little sign of abating, is a strong propensity for violence. If you insult a southerner—or, far worse, his wife, mother, or sister—you had better be very swift and profuse in your apologies, or he will vent his rage in violent assault on your person. The assault may be with his fists, which he knows well how to handle, having had to use them frequently in the maintenance of honor since he was a small boy. But it is also possible—and by no means uncommon—for him to "call you out" to settle the matter with firearms at close range.

There no longer is all that ritual about challenges and seconds, nor is the word "duel" often used. Western movies and television have made their imprint: the word today is "shoot-out." But the reality has undergone little change since the days before the Civil War, when outraged southern gentlemen faced each other at dawn with pistols or swords.

Within weeks after we came to Coontail Lagoon to live, the Aiken *Standard* carried a news item about two men who got into a quarrel in a downtown beer joint over a relatively trivial matter. Unforgivable words were spoken and they adjourned by mutual consent to the street outside, where each drew his pistol and shot the other. Both wounds proved to be fatal, thus sparing the courts the necessity of determining which of them might have been acting in self-defense.

While such episodes do not occur daily, they are sufficiently commonplace to explain why it is not New York, Los Angeles, Washington, or Detroit, but the census area embracing Aiken County and nearby Augusta, Georgia, that perennially leads the nation in per capita homicide rates.

Contributing to our high homicide rate is the attitude that southern juries are apt to take toward situations in which an unfaithful husband or wife is caught *in flagrante delicto* by the wronged spouse. The ventilation of the erring mate and his or her paramour by .38-caliber pistol bullets is considered, in such cases, not only justifiable but practically *de rigueur*. It is significant, I think, that southern audiences found little hilarity in the motion picture

Divorce—Italian Style. They had ambivalent emotions about it, being torn between empathy for the wronged husband, portrayed by Marcello Mastroianni, and a feeling that he was rather a bounder.

I will refer you to Mr. Cash's excellent book or other learned dissertations on southern history and its imprint on character for an explanation of this streak of violence that lies just below the gracious surface of southern behavior. My own theory, based on recollections of things I was taught as a child, is that it is a survival of the medieval code of honor, which had (and, to the extent that it still exists, still has) a large component of touchy personal pride.

To refuse battle, even with a person certain to batter or perhaps kill you, is regarded in the South as plain cowardice. And most southerners would vastly prefer to die honorably than to live as a coward.

This, of course, explains why the South rushed recklessly, almost insouciantly, into a self-destructive war against the Union. It also explains why the South has contributed far more than its proportional share of fighting men to every war in which the United States has subsequently been involved—including the Vietnam war.

I know for a fact that many young southerners—my own son was among them—went into combat in Vietnam with deep misgivings about the justice or necessity of American involvement in that conflict. I suspect many young southerners—including my great-grandfather, who lost an arm at Antietam—saw that "states' rights" was a politician's euphemism for preservation of the disgraceful institution of slavery. They went to war, not because they believed in the ostensible "cause," but out of a profound sense of duty, drilled into them from birth, which insists that no able-bodied man may ever refuse to answer a summons from his government to bear arms.

Some, in the climate of disillusionment created by Vietnam, may find this a dangerous, even reprehensible trait. But you would not think so had you ever stood lonely nighttime guard on a defense perimeter, taking comfort from the knowledge that the boy protecting your flank was a southerner, who would keep firing until he ran out of ammunition—even if your position were attacked by an entire enemy division. Until military force ceases to be a factor in international relations, a nation has need of men who have been conditioned by their culture to fight to the death rather than run. Without such troops, no battles are won. And it is the South, in this sense the Sparta of America, that consistently produces such troops for U.S. wars.

YOUNG PEOPLE tend to equate change with progress, while their elders are apt to fall into the equal and opposite error of regarding all change with apprehension. The truth is that some changes are good and some are bad.

Since my return to the South, I have become increasingly aware of one particular change that has taken place since I moved away some thirty-five years ago, a change that is undeniably for the better. It concerns the way black people live, the rights they enjoy, and the treatment they receive.

I realize that a great deal already has been written about race relations in the South. My excuse for adding another dissertation on this well-worked subject is a conviction that much of what has been published in the past has been sheer bilge. Either it has been written by white southerners who are eager to wallow in self-reproach or, conversely, eager to slip in an apologia for the way things used to be; or it has come from self-exiled blacks who are aware that the case for "compensatory treatment" of blacks—i.e., reverse racial discrimination—is best advanced by honing to a fine edge the guilt that any conscientious white person must feel.

As a white southerner I can hardy claim a detached view

of this matter. But I have had more than thirty years experience as a wire service reporter in the difficult discipline of setting aside my own prides, prejudices, and preconceptions in order to present all sides of a complex situation as honestly, objectively, and impartially as possible. And that is what I shall attempt to do in this report.

Forty years ago black people in the South were exploited, mistreated, and humiliated to a degree that shocked me even as a bewildered child. With the whole nation in the grip of an economic depression that was especially severe in rural agricultural areas of the South, blacks were relegated to field-hand work on farms, for which they received extremely low wages. My recollection is that the standard pay for a twelve-hour day of "chopping cotton" (i.e., hoeing the weeds out of it) was seventy-five cents. In harvest season a skilled cotton picker with the endurance to work in a bent-over position from dawn to dusk might earn as much as three dollars a day.

A few blacks managed to find nonfarm employment, but it was nearly always in menial jobs involving heavy physical labor—in lumber mills, on highway construction crews, as freight handlers, or as domestic servants.

The status of the latter particularly has been romanticized in much southern literature. I can confirm that there was in our home, and I'm sure there was in many others, a degree of mutual affection between white family and black servants which was, considering the circumstances, quite remarkable. But, I would have to add, it also was my firsthand observation that black servants worked very hard for very low pay. And some of them, at least, had to put up with a great deal of patronizing condescension, which must have quietly enraged them.

Black people generally lived in one- or two-room wooden shacks, unpainted and unscreened, roofed with corrugated iron and heated by a single open fireplace that was apt to be rather smoky. They got water from long-handled pitcher pumps, which usually needed a lot of priming before they caught. Their toilets were backyard privies. They did their laundry by boiling their clothes with brown-colored "lye soap" in big iron washtubs.

The segregated schools which black children attended were so far from being equal to white schools it is difficult to comprehend how it could have taken the Supreme Court until 1954 to acknowledge the gross injustice of the South's dual school system. It took rare ability for a black child to rise above the level of bare literacy—and many didn't even make it that far, even though they spent several years in school. Most black children left school by their middle teens to go to work.

From my own observation, and from what I have been told by black friends, the deprivations of black life in that era were not as galling as the humiliations. A white man— no matter how coarse, ignorant, filthy or dishonest—was likely to consider himself superior to any black man, and many arrogantly insisted that blacks acknowledge their inferior status by baring their heads and muttering innumerable "sirs" or "ma'ams" in any conversation with a white person.

A fat-bloated white farmer could with impunity slap a hard-muscled black field hand—who could have broken him in two with his bare hands had he not been deterred by the certain knowledge that retribution by the white man's law officers (or worse, by a white mob) would be swift and terrible. We still had lynchings in the South during my boyhood, and no aspect of them was more unspeakably evil than the grisly satisfaction that some whites took in "teaching niggers a lesson."

A white society terrified of the potential of black wrath

systematically resorted to terror to keep that wrath bottled up. It is ironic indeed that the blowup, when it came at last, took place mainly in urban centers of the North and West, far from the place where the fermenting grapes of wrath were bottled. I covered most of the big ghetto riots of the 1960's for UPI, and I discovered that many of my fellow newsmen were puzzled by the intensity of the fury which caused black people to burn and pillage. I was not in the least puzzled. I knew what black people were angry about, and how long they had waited for a chance to register their determination not to put up with any more of it. I simply wondered how they had stood it as long as they did.

Partly because of the ghetto riots—which had a far more salutary effect on white attitudes, North and South, than has been generally recognized; partly because of the federal civil rights legislation that began to emerge from a reluctant Congress under the needling of the feisty little man from Missouri, Harry S Truman; and partly because industrialization has created improved job opportunities, the situation of southern blacks has changed so dramatically for the better in recent years that I can scarcely believe what I see and hear in South Carolina today.

I see black and white children, in approximately equal numbers, peaceably attending schools which are so truly integrated that no federal court has found it necessary to order busing for racial balance. (In his 1972 Presidential campaign, before it was tragically aborted by a gunman, Governor George Wallace of Alabama found busing to be a much hotter issue in places such as Flint, Michigan, than it was in the South. The reason was that most of the South already had bitten the bullet and accepted school integration. It is mainly in the urban North that die-hard attempts still are being made to avoid it.)

Not only do I see black people voting in large numbers

(they constituted more than a third of the voters in South Carolina's last elections); I also see them running for office and *getting elected.* For the first time since Reconstruction there are black people in the South Carolina legislature and on the governing boards of our cities and counties. Most significant of all as a symbol of growing black political power, the South Carolina Democratic Party, which in my youth officially barred blacks from participating in its primaries, now has a black vice-chairman.

I see black men and women working in factories side by side with white men and women—for identical wages. I see black families living in modern brick homes and driving late-model cars. I see black people sitting where they choose in movie theaters, entering restaurants and motels without qualms. I do *not* see rest rooms, waiting rooms, and water fountains labeled "colored" and "white."

The evidence of my ears, if possible, is even more difficult to believe: it sounds too good to be true. But I believe it is true, because it comes from black people as well as whites.

I hear white people—even those of relatively low economic station and little education—routinely according to black people the courtesy titles of "Mr.," "Mrs.," or "Miss."

I hear southern politicians cultivating black voters with ringing words about racial equality—words that would have meant instant political suicide in the atmosphere of "white supremacy" which dominated southern elections less than a generation ago.

I hear black people—including many whose militancy in the cause of racial rights has been proven beyond question—saying that race relations in the South today are much farther advanced toward the goal of easy and natural equality than in any urban area of the North or West.

Lewis Robinson is a black man who grew up in Decatur, Alabama. He has lived most of his adult life in northern cities, principally Cleveland, Ohio. He is more than a militant; he is genuine revolutionary, in the sense of being committed to racial equality without regard to what it may cost him personally, or how much turmoil may have to be created in society in order to achieve it. After the Cleveland riot of 1966, in which he played an important role, he and I became sufficiently well acquainted to talk truthfully to each other about race relations.

He told me he felt that the southern white's attitude toward blacks—even in his childhood (which was contemporary with my own)—has always been a "great deal better," from a black person's viewpoint, than the attitudes he encounters among whites of the North and West.

"There is less hypocrisy about race in the South," he said. "A southern bigot talks and acts like a bigot. You know where you stand with him. A northern bigot often tries to sound like a speaker at a civil rights rally.

"Even in the old days, there were southern whites— quite a lot of them, actually—who treated black people with respect, who were genuinely well disposed toward us. You knew they meant it because they were bucking all the pressure of their culture to treat you decently. I think these white people were tremendously relieved when federal courts, and civil rights laws, and the general course of events made it 'necessary' for them to do what they'd always felt in their hearts they ought to do: namely, treat black people as fellow human beings.

"There certainly were many white southerners—there still are a great many—who have found it all but impossible to adjust to the idea of black equality in an unsegregated society. But for the most part these last-ditchers are what black people call 'buckras'—meaning lower-class whites. They seem to fulfill some psychological need by referring to us, among themselves anyway, as 'niggers.'

"But I think there was a great reservoir just waiting to be tapped in the South—a reservoir of goodwill toward blacks among whites who had suffered a long time from a guilty conscience about the injustice of the old ways.

"Now, in northern cities, I find an entirely different situation. Most white people in the North have never known black people on any sort of personal, human level—as nearly all southern whites have. The northern white is committed—verbally anyway—to the principle that black people are entitled to economic and political equality.

"But he doesn't want to associate with us, or have his children go to school with ours, because he's afraid of us. He sees us as abstractions, not people, and he's scared to death of the crime, disease, and poverty he associates with his stereotype of black men.

"Frankly, I'd rather deal with a bigoted southern white man than a scared northern white man any day. The 'race problem' is gradually disappearing in the South—not fast enough to suit me, but faster than I had dared to hope. In northern cities, it is getting worse—much faster than white people realize."

I have quoted Lewis Robinson at length because I think this is a subject on which only a black man can speak with authority—and because he is one of the wisest and most courageous men I've ever known. For what it's worth, as a white man who has lived both in the South and in the North, I agree completely with his observations.

I HAVE FOUND since coming home that the South's favorite sports are the same today as they were in my youth. They are—in order of popularity—politics and fishing. Contrary to what might be regarded in other parts of the country as an appropriate attitude, southerners take fishing very seriously, while their approach to politics is characterized by a good deal of levity.

The Watergate scandals, which caused such consternation in most of America, were followed in the South with fascinated attention, as any political development is. But there was relatively little shock evident among southern politician-watchers as Senator Sam Ervin and his colleagues brought forth on national television disclosure after disclosure of hanky-panky in high places. Southerners take for granted that all politicians are apt to be crooked unless very closely watched—an attitude which this battle-weary Washington correspondent regards as healthy and realistic.

As one of my friends remarked during the Watergate hearings, "every politician knows that it pays to be honest —but it don't pay as much."

One of the conspicuous changes that have occurred in southern politics in recent years, as I mentioned in the previous chapter, is the advent of the Negro vote as a factor which every office seeker must take into account. Few spectacles have provided more quiet amusement to observant politician-watchers than the frantic scramble of septuagenarian Senator Strom Thurmond, in his 1972 campaign for reelection, to reach what one of his campaign aides indiscreetly called "high ground on this racial issue."

Thurmond, who once ran for president as a States' Rights candidate pledged to bitter-end defense of segregation, emerged in 1972 in the role of best friend of the black man. He won reelection, with the aid of a baby born to him by his youthful beauty queen wife at just the right time and despite some acidulous comments about deathbed conversion on the race question.

At one political rally which I attended, a member of the audience, a white farmer who evidently preferred Thurmond's original stance on segregation, raised a question as to whether President Nixon, in pressing for school integration in the South despite Thurmond's past assurances to white voters that he would do no such thing, had "made a fool of 'Ol' Strom.' "

Quick as a flash, the speaker—who happened to be a Democrat—replied:

"Oh, no. I don't know who made a fool of Strom, but the job was completed long before Nixon became President."

Even Thurmond supporters in the crowd laughed uproariously. A good political joke is always appreciated in the South—even if it's at the expense of your candidate.

The southern code of honor requires that a politician take immediate and, if necessary, violent exception to any public statement by an opponent which may seem to impugn his integrity. This touchiness was even more pronounced, perhaps, in my childhood than it is today.

I remember a tale my father used to tell—and this one

108

rings true—about a race for county sheriff. The incumbent, wearing a large pistol, arrived one evening at the home of his opponent in the election. "Will," said the sheriff, "I hear you been going around telling folks that I am a liar, a thief, and a cowardly son of a bitch."

"That's not true, sheriff," Will replied, hefting the shotgun he had brought with him when he answered the door. "I never told anybody those things about you. I don't know how people found out."

One other major change in southern politics—besides the disappearance of overt racism as a feature of campaign oratory—has taken place in southern politics during my exile in the North. We now have Republicans. In fact, vote tallies lately indicate that we often have more Republicans than Democrats in South Carolina, especially in Aiken County.

From conversation and observation, I have concluded that many whites and some middle-class blacks have become outspoken Republicans out of a vague feeling that it is a hallmark of upward social mobility. I suspect that Abraham Lincoln would share my feeling that this is a poor reason for being a Republican. But at least it has helped to give the South a two-party system, which it certainly needed.

In my youth, Republicans were so scarce in South Carolina they were regarded as curiosities, rather like two-headed calves. The only contest that mattered was the Democratic primary. General elections were widely ignored.

An exception to this rule was the Presidential election of 1928, when many southerners were sorely tempted to commit the heresy of voting Republican (for Herbert Hoover) rather than cast their ballots for a Democratic candidate (Alfred E. Smith) who had publicly admitted being a Catholic and favoring the repeal of prohibition.

I was a boy of seven at the time, and already as keenly interested in politics as any true southerner. My father, who had been appointed an election supervisor for our voting precinct in Ellenton, allowed me to tag along after him when he went to the polling place, located in an empty gasoline service station. We arrived early in the morning of election day. It was brisk for early November and the other election supervisor, Mr. Dixie Dunbar, had started a roaring fire in a pot-bellied iron stove which stood in one corner of the room.

After exchanging greetings—they were old and close friends—my father and Mr. Dunbar went over to inspect the election materials. They included, naturally, a stack of Republican ballots. (In those days, in the South anyway, you didn't mark a ballot in secret: you just asked for the "ticket" of the party of your choice and dropped it into the tin ballot box.)

"Mike," said Mr. Dunbar reflectively, "do you realize there has never been a single Republican ballot cast in the Ellenton precinct since Reconstruction?"

"Yes," said my father. "But I'm afraid today will spoil our record. I hear a lot of people talking about voting for Hoover."

They brooded over this impending disgrace for several minutes.

"There could be an accident," Mr. Dunbar observed.

"There sure could," said my father, reading him loud and clear. "If you'll open that stove door, I'll make sure there is one."

Mr. Dunbar opened the stove door and my father tossed into the fire all the Republican ballots. The sanctity of the Ellenton ballot box was preserved. Our town went solidly Democratic in 1928 because it was quite literally the only way to go.

My father and Mr. Dunbar did not live to see Republicans win elections in South Carolina. I suppose I should be reticent about confessing their flagrant violation of election laws. But they are now beyond the reach of federal prosecutors and I doubt that either of them would really mind my telling how strongly they felt about saving Ellenton from the ignominy of having Republican votes appear in its box.

Until the day of his death in 1957, my father continued to regard voting Republican as a sin comparable to, or worse than, incest or grand larceny. But he managed to retain his sense of humor even about his own political prejudices. One Sunday my mother, a devoted Baptist, was performing the ancient rite of serving dinner to a visiting preacher, a gentleman even more suspicious of newfangled ways than was my father. Recognizing in his guest a narrowness of viewpoint vastly exceeding his own (actually, my father was quite open-minded on all issues except voting Republican), he decided to needle the old preacher a bit.

Since I was working in Washington at the time, I wasn't present at the table, but my younger sister was.

"Is this your only child?" inquired the minister, in what he doubtless thought an entirely safe conversational gambit.

My father, instead of replying, hung his head and stared at his plate. This bit of ham-acting alerted my mother and sister to expect some outrageous comment from him, and they had not long to wait.

"Well, Reverend," he finally said, "we did have a son too. But we no longer mention his name in this house."

"Oh, I'm terribly sorry," said the clergyman, embarrassed at having opened a painful subject, but also overcome by curiosity. "What is the trouble with your son?"

"I forgave him when he married a Yankee," said my father gravely. "I even forgave him when he voted Republican. But now he has turned Episcopalian."

The Baptist minister could find no words of comfort to offer my father in the face of this ultimate tragedy. He hung his own head and stared silently at his plate, while my mother and sister found excuses to flee into the kitchen and collapse in laughter.

In point of fact, I am not at all sure that my father could have forgiven me very easily had he known for sure that I had cast a Republican ballot. But he adored his Yankee daughter-in-law, whom he frequently introduced as "the only smart thing Louis ever did." And he certainly didn't mind my being an Episcopalian. On the contrary, he was a strong believer in interreligious harmony long before anyone heard the word "ecumenism."

One of his proudest moments was the day when some Jewish friends with whom he'd had close business relations for many years sent him a packet of unleavened bread and other materials for celebrating a seder at the beginning of Passover. With the packet came a letter, duly signed by a rabbi, proclaiming him an "honorary Jew."

While virtually all southerners are fascinated with politics, only an overwhelming majority are fishermen. I suppose I should make that "fisherpersons." Some of the ablest and most fanatical anglers I know are women.

Among the first possessions a young southerner wishes to acquire, as soon as he has a job to pay for them, are (1) a bass boat, with outboard motor, that can be hauled on a two-wheeled trailer; (2) the trailer; and (3) a pickup truck, preferably with a camper roof over the rear section, in which he can unroll a sleeping bag at night. He does not need to purchase fishing tackle: he has had that since he was a toddler. But after he has made his initial acquisitions of boat, trailer, and truck, he may blow the next few weeks' pay on a new rod and spinner and a few other essential gadgets such as four dozen assorted bass lures, none of which will work half as well as a rubber worm.

When all requisite equipment is in hand, including adequate supplies of potables and mosquito repellent, the fisherman and one or two carefully chosen companions set forth, well before dawn, for a lake or river. In South Carolina, we have several great fishing lakes, including Clark Hill on the Savannah River, Lake Murray near Columbia, and the twin lakes (Marion and Moultrie) formed in the low-country swamps by construction of the Santee-Cooper hydroelectric power and flood control dam. Each fisherman has his favorite body of water, and a favorite location within that body of water. He takes an exceedingly dim view of any intruder who happens to beat him to what he regards as "my spot."

One fisherman made the newspapers a while back when he became so outraged at an interloper that he charged his boat full speed into the other boat, with disastrous consequences to both vessels. Fortunately, this sort of thing does not happen very often. Most fishermen will, out of courtesy or prudence, vacate immediately any stretch of water which another fisherman claims as his personal "spot."

Although folklore maintains that all anglers are notorious liars when describing the magnitude of their catches, I have not observed this phenomenon among truly dedicated southern fishermen, a category which includes a large percentage of the total population. To these disciples of Izaak Walton, fishing is much too serious a matter to lie about or even to joke about. (Offhand, fishing and the virtue of his wife are the only two subjects I can think of that nearly every southerner regards as unfit topics for humorous comment.)

The earnestness of the southern fisherman may derive,

in part at least, from the fact that he does not think of fishing primarily as a sport or hobby. Its first purpose is to put food on the table—and very delightful food it is, when the catch consists of bass, bream, shellcrackers, rockfish or any of several other game fish varieties that are found in great quantity in southern lakes and rivers. Catching fish is only half the joy of fishing. Ultimate fulfillment awaits the hour when the catch is cleaned, cooked, and consumed, preferably by a campfire on the shore.

Since a good fisherman usually can catch in a day's fishing far more than he or his immediate companions can eat on the spot, ice chests are taken along to transport the excess home, where it will be placed in a freezer. Unfortunately, the truly ardent fisherman can fill a freezer much more rapidly than his family can empty it, which compels his frantic wife to begin giving fish away to any neighbor, friend, or stranger who will accept the donation. Lining up a recipient may present difficulties, because most of the housewives to whom the surplus is proffered already have their own freezers full of fish. My Uncle Arthur, a fisherman of rare skill and single-minded determination, solved this disposal problem by buying a new freezer each time the one he had been using reached its storage capacity. I forget how many he ended up with, but it was more than you'd find in the average appliance store, and they were all full of fish.

Why not give the surplus fish to poor families? I can assure you that was the first idea that would have occurred to Uncle Arthur, who was a generous and compassionate man. But it really isn't a solution, because fishing is the favorite outdoor activity of all economic groups in the South, and the less-than-affluent are perfectly able and more than willing to catch their own.

PART
IV

Wake Up, Bug Out, and Live

CHAPTER

15

THE READER who has persisted to this point must have observed that the pattern of this book, if projected schematically, would consist of three concentric circles.

The first part, which represents the smallest, innermost circle, is entirely preoccupied with Coontail Lagoon and what we've learned from living here about the infinitely fascinating world of nature.

My wife says she can detect in this first section something I was not at all conscious of putting there: my rediscovery of the simple joy of being alive, as I moved slowly and gingerly back from the brink of death. What I see as I reread it is a rather surprised response to the beauty of God's world by a man who had hitherto been too busy to notice it.

The short-radius circle of Part I was not the result of a deliberate plan. It simply reflects the fact that these chapters were written during the early months of convalescence, when my physical activity was so sharply circumscribed that I had to remain close to home.

In Part II—and again, this is something I didn't plan or even realize until it was written—the circle is somewhat larger. It is wide enough to include the entire community in which we live, and it reflects the excitement, amusement, and affection that I experienced after I was able to get about to explore Aiken and participate in its extraordinarily rich and busy life.

In Part III, the circle has expanded to include not merely home and community but also region: the changing South. Again, this was not preplanned. It also reflects a progressive physical recovery that enabled me to resume a newspaperman's lifetime habit of observing and caring about people and the way they live and organize their society.

Now I shall attempt to draw the circle even wider—to include you: whoever you are, wherever you live, whatever plans you may have for your future. In this chapter I want to reflect on our Coontail Lagoon adventure in an effort to identify what it has taught us that may have universal application to all human beings who are trying to find joy, peace, and meaning in life.

Our tastes, of course, are not necessarily your tastes, and our conclusions may not be valid for you. I can only suggest that you try them on for size, regarding them as one couple's reaction to the experience of embarking on a new life-style in middle age. If you find anything that seems to make sense to you or to answer some of your existential questions, I hope you'll test it in the laboratory of your own life. That's the only way to find out what will work for you.

Our first conclusion (I presume to speak for Charlotte as well as myself because we have discussed these things for many hours and see pretty much eye to eye about them) is that a seeming disaster, such as a serious illness, may turn out to be a great boon if it compels you to reappraise the way of life into which ambition and accident have led you. You need not wait for a personal cataclysm to form this reappraisal. Anyone can and we believe *everyone* should call time-out occasionally to consider what he really wants out

118

of life. Are you genuinely happy—not *all* the time, of course (no one can expect that), but ever? There are trials, frustrations, and harassments in any kind of life. Does yours now include, in addition to these inevitable bad times, at least some moments of joy and peace and laughter? If the answer is no, you ought to consider the possibility of starting afresh, trying to make a new life in a new place under new circumstances, with new objectives.

If you seriously propose to seek a new and fuller life, the first step toward it—in our experience, at least—is to rid yourself entirely of the almost universal assumption of our society that "success" is the proper goal of human existence. We have come to doubt whether the pursuit of success is compatible with the pursuit of happiness, and we are quite certain the two are not synonymous.

Renouncing success as a life objective is not merely a philosophical exercise. It may have traumatic dollars-and-cents consequences. High income is the bait our society uses to keep its weary rats racing. If you are fed up with the race —and the effect it has on your health, your marriage, your relationship with your children, or your capacity for enjoyment of life—you must be prepared to forgo the bait.

We accepted a drastic cut in income when we moved to Coontail Lagoon, and our optimistic assumption that living costs would be much cheaper here has not proved entirely realistic. But to anyone weighing a comparable decision, we can say unequivocally that no amount of money would induce us to return to our old way of life.

Once you've tried both, there'll be no doubt in your mind that it's much better to *live* on a budget than to "live it up" on an expense account.

If earning maximum income is not to be your objective, what criteria shall you use in deciding what kind of job or career to pursue? Two things seem to us to be of crucial importance. First, your daily work should be something you *enjoy* doing. This doesn't mean it will be devoid of drudgery: no job is. But it should offer you the satisfaction of feeling, at least occasionally, that you have done a good piece of work in a field in which you have natural talent or developed skills. Work, even very hard work, if it is the right sort, can be more pleasurable than many of the hectic activities that people pursue in the name of "fun."

The second test for a job or career is whether it gives you an opportunity to make a contribution to your community or to humanity in general. One of the most valuable insights of today's young generation, which their parents desperately need to apply to their own lives, is that the psychological rewards of a job are directly proportional to what might be called the service quotient of the work involved. Are you helping others, hurting them, or just trying to milk them? It makes a difference in how you feel at the end of a day.

Or at least, it *should* make a difference, and if you can no longer feel that difference, something is dying inside you and you ought to see what you can do about resuscitating it.

What you decide to do will have an important bearing on *where* you can do it. I am cognizant of the fact that a writer has a considerable advantage over many other people in deciding to pull up stakes and move out of the smog, traffic congestion, overcrowding, and consequent mutual irritation of big-city life. The type of work you want to do or feel best qualified to do (basically the same thing, I believe) may compel you to live in a metropolitan area. But there are a lot more types of work than you may realize which are now available in—or within easy commuting range of—small towns.

If you can manage by any means to find fulfilling work in a nonurban area, we strongly recommend that you do so. We have been at Coontail Lagoon long enough to get a full picture of the differences between big-city and small-town life. While there are some points at which urban living must be credited with clear advantages, there is no question in our minds that the overall balance is overwhelmingly in favor of what former Secretary of Agriculture Orville Freeman liked to call "town-and-country America."

We lived for nearly three decades in New York and Washington. We still miss, and probably shall always continue to miss, the variety of choice we had in those great cities when we wanted to see a play or movie, listen to a concert, or watch a television program. In Aiken, we have two movie theaters, one of which thinks "R" is the only letter in the alphabet. We can receive programs broadcast by two television stations in nearby Augusta, neither of which has an adequate appreciation of the audience appeal of the Washington Redskins. So we spend a lot of evenings reading. Fortunately, we both like to read. This is one pleasure that is as widely and readily available in a small town as a big city.

When we first came, we felt deprived in the matter of shopping, especially for clothing and home furnishings. But that problem has been solved by the opening of an interstate highway that allows us to drive from Coontail Lagoon to downtown Atlanta in less than three hours. We do this fairly often, usually remaining overnight so that we not only can shop at stores such as Saks, Lord & Taylor, and Neiman-Marcus but also can enjoy the rich diet of entertainment and cultural activities offered in this fast-growing regional capital, which now has a population of nearly two million.

I mention this because a study of the map indicates that the United States has thousands of genuine small towns (as opposed to suburbs, which are a different breed of cat altogether) which are within comparable driving range of cities as large as Atlanta. You could live in any of these

121

towns without giving up the most attractive amenity of urban life, namely, the accessibility of a large number of excellent shops, restaurants, and theaters.

Whatever inconvenience or expense may be entailed in driving two hours to your "shopping city" must be weighed against the realization that it takes about half that much time nowadays just to get downtown from a big-city suburb.

Also, the fact that you live at a substantial distance from metropolitan traffic congestion greatly reduces the time required for you to get from your home to the mountains, the seashore, a lake, or some other outdoor recreation spot. We spend many more days tooling around Lake Murray in my speedy little powerboat than we do shopping in Atlanta; so the balance is heavily in our favor in the matter of how long it takes to get where we want to go. I think this would be equally true for a vast number of towns, especially in the eastern half of the country and along the Pacific coast.

While we are on the subject of shopping, I must mention another conspicuous advantage we've observed in small-town life. The people who serve the public—as police officers, bus drivers, bank tellers, garage mechanics, appliance repairmen, or what have you—are much more courteous and obliging than their counterparts in a big city. Servicemen actually tell you when they'll be there—and come on time—instead of expecting you to remain at home all day, or for days on end, awaiting the hour when it may be entirely convenient for them to attend to your problem. I do not know exactly why this difference exists, but my working hypothesis is that urban life is driving everyone involved into the state of nervous tension and mutual hostility that psychologists have observed in experiments with rats living in severely overcrowded cages. The rats vent their frustrations by snarling and snapping at each other, in a manner remarkably reminiscent of New York taxi drivers.

To one who has had extensive firsthand acquaintance with the ways in which excessive population density blights urban life, it is a bit shocking to find state and local government agencies in underpopulated areas such as the South engaged in fevered competition for more industry and more population.

Some of these areas doubtless need additional factories and people to reach an optimum level of economic activity. But the pursuit of growth for growth's sake is one of the most shortsighted policies a state or town can pursue. It is plain stupid to throw away the blessings of life in an uncrowded, smog-free environment in order to achieve the dubious benefit of being able to report an impressive annual increment in population or the acquisition of a new factory. But a large part of town-and-country America is currently enmeshed precisely in this folly, and probably cannot be deterred from it so long as our national mores elevate "success" to the supreme position in our scale of values.

So far I have argued that living in town-and-country America can be a lot more pleasant than living in urban areas (where two out of three Americans now live, or exist). If you accept this thesis, and if you are in, or can switch to, a field of employment that is not necessarily riveted to an urban address, what then? How do you decide exactly when and where to move?

As for when, that's easy to answer. Now. The sooner the better. Each day you postpone it, the harder it will become to take the gamble of breaking out of your present rut—and the less of your life will be left for real living.

Moreover, as a practical consideration, the exodus from the urban jungle already has begun, and the earlier you join it, the better will be your chances of finding the place you want at a price you can afford.

In some of the most desirable town-and-country areas,

such as our own Aiken County, land prices are rising rapidly as the influx of city refugees grows. Wild, unspoiled forest land, especially if it is on or near water, now costs five times as much per acre as it did just a few years ago when we were shopping for our swamp. By urban standards, acreage is still remarkably cheap out here in the happy hinterlands. Buy now, before it gets any higher.

In choosing your small town (please don't come to Aiken —we already have plenty of people here), your first test should be: is it dying or coming to life? Every small town I have visited seems to be moving quite distinctly in one direction or the other. You can sense in a fairly short visit whether a particular town is sliding slowly into moribundity or beginning to throb with fresh vitality. Growth, though I deplore it when there is too much of it, is a sign of vitality. Try to find a place that is growing, but not growing too fast for its own good.

We chose the South because we feel at home here, and because it is an area that is growing at a healthy rate and still has room for considerably more growth before it develops the disease of urbanitis.

However, I suggest you take a look at all sections of town-and-country America, paying particular attention to the region where you lived as a child. In spite of the fantastic degree of mobility that has become characteristic of American life, there still are such things as "roots," and they are more important, psychologically, than most people realize. See if you can find a place where you feel that you have, or could put down, roots. If you have family or friends already living there, or even a few acquaintances who will introduce you into community life, count that a big plus.

I think it is desirable if not essential, for reasons previously indicated, that your place be far enough away from a metropolitan area to be a true small town in its own right rather than a suburb, which is locked into urban modes of life, even as its name indicates. But you should seek a place not more than two or three hours by car from a city with a population of at least five hundred thousand—preferably one million—people. With the spread of the interstate highway system, this gives you a number of fairly wide circles within which to search. Mark them out on a highway map with a geometry compass, and devote one or two vacations to exploring the areas you find most appealing.

You will recognize your town when you find it. It must have a job you can do. It should be alive and growing, but still uncrowded. You will want to make sure it has adequate schools and medical facilities—they are the really crucial needs—and a public library. The latter is not technically indispensable in this day of mail-order book buying, but I have a strong conviction that a town without a library, however modest, lacks not only one of the amenities of, but also the instinct for, civilized living.

I think you will be pleasantly surprised, if you undertake this kind of search, by the number of small or medium-sized towns in the less-populated regions of America that do have good schools, good doctors, and good libraries. I suspect you will be downright amazed by the number that have symphony orchestras, ballet schools, and community theaters. I repeat: the bug-out from the city has already begun and in the vanguard, as usual, are talented and interesting people who believe that *quality* is as much a dimension of life, and an even more important one, than quantity.

If you decide after careful deliberation that the nature of your work, or the demands of your children's education, or simply your own preferences, tie you inextricably to the city, there still are things you can do to improve the quality of your life there. You might consider moving from the suburbs back into a rehabilitated section of the core city. The notion that suburbs provide children with a healthful "greenbelt" environment is pure bunk. The main effect of suburban life is to subject the mothers of younger children to an impossible schedule of ceaseless chauffeuring, while sentencing fathers to a lifetime of dreary commuting through everdenser traffic jams. As for the children, they reach their teens, not with a carefree love of nature, but with a passionate desire to have a car of their own so they can get into town, where the action is.

Whether you move all the way into the city or continue to inhabit its overrated and overpriced suburban fringe, please do whatever you can, through conscious planning and deliberate cultivation of new habits, to simplify your life. Unclutter your schedule at least enough to allow time for occasional visits to the nearest stretch of park or open country in which you can find some degree of unspoiled nature.

Become a bird-listener. Get acquainted with wildflowers. Sit by a rushing stream and try to sort out the component sounds of its intricate music. Despite all that man has done to uglify and pollute the world, there remain enormous areas where beauty still abounds, where the air is pure and the water runs swift and clean.

I wish you could live in such a setting all the time, as we do. But at the very least, you can refresh your mind, soul, and body with periodic visits to places where you can sense what the old hymn meant: "This is my Father's world."

Indeed it is. And he meant us not merely to endure living in it, but to enjoy it.